AMERICAN SCHOOL OF NEEDLEWORK
PRESENTS

THE GREAT AFGHAN BOOK

President: Jean Leinhauser
Editorial Director: Mary Thomas
Art Director: Carol Wilson Mansfield
Art Assistant: Julie A. Ryan
Operations Vice President: Irmgard Barnes
Book Coordinator-Production Manager: Robert J. Kasbar
Photography by Stemo Photography Inc., Northbrook, IL
Roderick A. Stemo, President
James E. Zorn, Photographer

CONTENTS

Published by Sterling Publishing Co., Inc.
Two Park Avenue, New York, N.Y. 10016
Distributed in Canada by Oak Tree Press Ltd.
% Canadian Manda Group, P.O. Box 920, Station U
Toronto, Ontario, Canada M8Z 5P9
Distributed in the United Kingdom by Blandford Press
Link House, West Street, Poole, Dorset BH15 1LL, England
Distributed in Australia by Capricorn Ltd.
P.O. Box 665, Lane Cove, NSW 2066
Manufactured in the United States of America
All rights reserved

We have made every effort to ensure the accuracy and completeness of the instructions in this book. We cannot, however, be responsible for human error, typographical mistakes or variations in individual work.

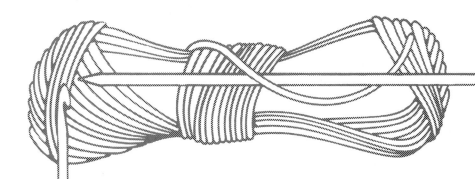

More afghans are knitted and crocheted each year in the United States than any other type of project.

Why this popularity?

Perhaps it is partly because afghans offer unlimited possibilities for combining colors and textures; because many afghan patterns are made up of small motifs or strips that are easily portable; because afghans don't have to fit anybody; because they make such welcome gifts; and because they provide warmth during the present day energy crisis.

Many a baby is christened wrapped lovingly in a hand-made lacy white blanket; toddlers snuggle up under a colorful afghan decorated with animals; teens may take a sturdy afghan to a beach party; the family room would not be complete without its afghan; and the elderly welcome a lightweight but warm afghan to spead over the knees.

In essence, today's afghan has assumed the role of yesterday's patchwork quilt. However, few needleworkers now have the time patiently to piece, then quilt, warm coverings for family and friends. Yet a knitted or crocheted afghan can be made quickly and easily— and inexpensively. Many afghans, such as the granny square, are designed to make use of yarn scraps that would otherwise be thrown away.

Today's afghans, then, will become tomorrow's heirlooms. And in this book we have tried to give you a wide selection of designs, both new and traditional, to tempt you to take up hook or needles and create your own masterpiece.

Jean Leinhauser

Jean Leinhauser
President
American School of Needlework, Inc.

ACKNOWLEDGMENTS

Our special thanks go to American Thread, the Boye Needle Co. and C. J. Bates & Son who provided us with several designs in this book.

We express our gratitude to the following pattern testers who made and tested the patterns in this book:

Irene Beitner, Berwyn, IL
Nannette M. Berkley, Antioch, IL
Penny Boswinkle, Libertyville, IL
Marge Connolly, Wilmette, IL
Judy Demain, Highland Park, IL
Lori Demain, Highland Park, IL
Eleanor Denner, Pontiac, MO
Judy Elsenbach, Evanston, IL
Joanne Fogarty, Kenilworth, IL
Peggy Fogarty, Kenilworth, IL
Diane Gorsline, Des Plaines, IL
Patricia K. Gorsline, Northbrook, IL
Kim Hubal, Evanston, IL
Joan Kokaska, Wildwood, IL
Kathy LaForge, Zion, IL
Jean Luitgaarden, Deerfield, IL
Barbara Luoma, Clearwater, FL
Betsy Meyers, Wilmette, IL
Margaret Miller, Chicago, IL
Elizabeth Mitzen, Glenview, IL
Fran Mueller, Libertyville, IL
Wanda Parker, Mundelein, IL
Patty Rankin, Minneapolis, MN
Kathie Schroeder, Tucson, AZ
Virginia Snite, Wilmette, IL
Rosemarie Suhr, McHenry, IL
Diane Vinti, Lake Villa, IL

We also acknowledge our thanks and appreciation to the following contributing designers:

Eleanor Denner, Pontiac, MO
Anis Duncan, Northbrook, IL
Doris England, Des Plaines, IL
Joan Harmon, Glen Ellyn, IL
Jean Leinhauser, Glenview, IL
Carol Wilson Mansfield, Northbrook, IL
Jane Cannon Meyers, Wilmette, IL
Wanda Parker, Mundelein, IL
Barbara A. Retzke, Libertyville, IL
Julie A. Ryan, Highland Park, IL
Grif Stenger, Northbrook, IL
Mary Thomas, Libertyville, IL
Verna Williams, Peoria Heights, IL

YARN SOURCES

We have given the brand name for any specialty yarn used in this book. If unable to find these yarns locally, write to the following manufacturers who can tell you where to purchase their product:

American Thread, High Ridge Park, Stamford, CT 08905
C.J. Bates & Son, Chester, CT 06412

Chapter 1

Afghan Basics

Here's a helpful review of the basics of knitting and crocheting, making fringe, and a listing of the abbreviations and symbols used in this book.

Instructions for working afghan stitch, broomstick lace and hairpin lace are given in the chapters on these special techniques.

KNITTING

Casting On (CO)

Only one knitting needle is used with this method. First, measure off a length of yarn that allows about 1″ for each stitch you are going to cast on. Make a slip knot on needle as follows. Make a yarn loop, leaving about 4″ length of yarn at free end; insert needle into loop and draw up yarn from free end to make a loop on needle **(Fig 1)**. Pull yarn firmly, but not tightly, to form a slip knot on needle **(Fig 2)**. This slip knot counts as your first stitch. Now work as follows.

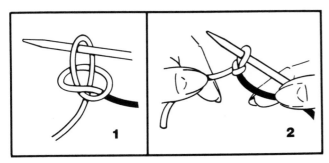

Step 1: Hold needle with slip knot in right hand, with yarn from skein to your right, and measured length of yarn to your left. With left hand, make a yarn loop **(Fig 3)** and insert needle into loop **(Fig 4)**.

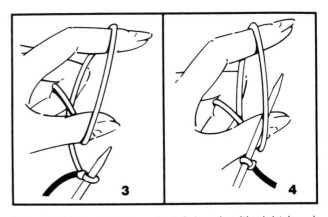

Step 2: Still holding loop in left hand; with right hand, pick up yarn from skein and bring it from back to front around the needle **(Fig 5)**.

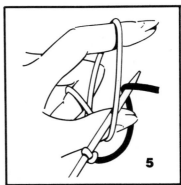

Step 3: Bring needle through loop and toward you; at the same time, pull gently on yarn end to tighten loop **(Fig 6)**. Make it snug but not tight below needle.

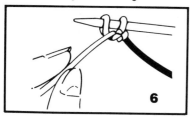

You now have one cast-on stitch. Repeat Steps 1 through 3 for each additional stitch desired.

The Knit Stitch (K)

Step 1: Hold the needle with cast-on stitches in your left hand. Insert point of right needle in first stitch, from left to right, just as in casting on **(Fig 7)**.

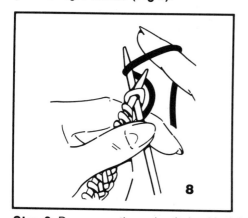

Step 2: With right index finger, bring yarn under and over point of right needle **(Fig 8)**.

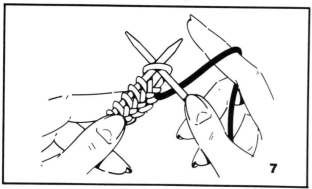

Step 3: Draw yarn through stitch with right needle point **(Fig 9)**.

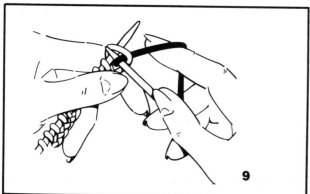

Step 4: Slip the loop on the left needle off, so the new stitch is entirely on the right needle **(Fig 10)**.

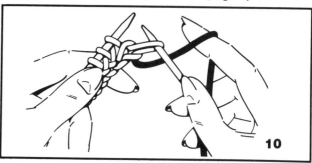

This completes one knit stitch.

The Purl Stitch (P)

The reverse of the knit stitch is called the purl stitch. Instead of inserting the right needle point from left to right under the left needle (as you did for the knit stitch), you will now insert it from right to left, in front of the left needle.

Step 1: Insert right needle, from right to left, into first stitch, and in front of left needle **(Fig 11)**.

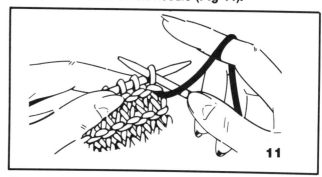

Step 2: Holding yarn in front of work (side toward you), bring it around right needle counterclockwise **(Fig 12)**.

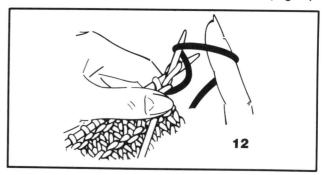

Step 3: With right needle, pull yarn back through stitch **(Fig 13)**. Slide stitch off left needle, leaving new stitch on right needle **(Fig 14)**.

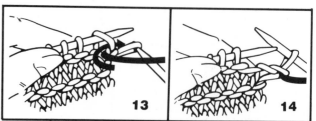

One purl stitch is now completed.

Binding Off (BO)
To bind off on the knit side:
Step 1: Knit the first 2 stitches. Then insert left needle into the first of the 2 stitches **(Fig 15)**, and pull it over the second stitch and completely off the needle **(Fig 16)**. You have now bound off one stitch.

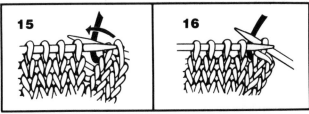

Step 2: Knit one more stitch; insert left needle into first stitch on right needle and pull it over the new stitch and completely off the needle **(Fig 17)**. Another stitch is now bound off.

Repeat Step 2 until all sts are bound off and one loop remains on right-hand needle. ''Finish off'' or ''end off'' the yarn (cut yarn and draw end through last loop).

To bind off on the purl side:
Step 1: Purl the first 2 stitches. Now insert left needle into the first stitch on right needle, and pull it over the second stitch and completely off the needle. You have now bound off one stitch.

Step 2: Purl one more stitch; insert left needle into first stitch on right needle and pull it over the new stitch and completely off the needle. Another stitch is bound off.

Repeat Step 2 until all sts are bound off.

Yarn Over (YO)
To make a yarn over before a knit stitch, bring yarn to front of work as if you were going to purl, then take it over the right needle to the back into the position for knitting; then knit the next stitch **(Fig 18)**.

To make a yarn over before a purl stitch, bring yarn around right needle from front to back, then back around into position for purling; purl the next stitch **(Fig 19)**.

CROCHETING

Chain (ch)
Crochet always starts with a basic chain. To begin, make a slip loop on hook **(Fig 20)**, leaving a 4″ tail of yarn.

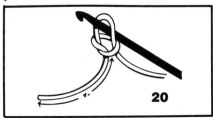

Step 1: Take hook in right hand, holding it between thumb and third finger **(Fig 21)**, and rest index finger near tip of hook.

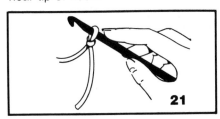

Step 2: Take slip loop in thumb and index finger of left hand **(Fig 22)** and bring yarn over third finger of left hand, catching it loosely at left palm with remaining two fingers.

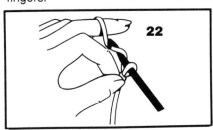

Step 3: Bring yarn over hook from back to front **(Fig 23)**, and draw through loop on hook.

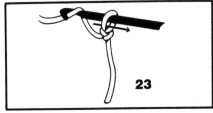

One chain made. Repeat Step 3 for each additional chain desired, moving your left thumb and index finger up close to the hook after each stitch or two **(Fig 24)**.

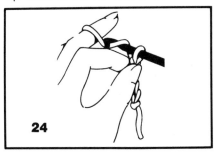

When counting number of chains, do not count the loop on the hook or the starting slip knot.

Single Crochet (sc)

First, make a chain to desired length.

Step 1: Insert hook in top loop of 2nd chain from hook **(Fig 25)**; hook yarn (bring yarn over hook from back to front) and draw through **(Fig 26)**.

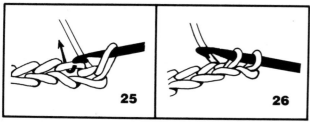

Step 2: Hook yarn and draw through 2 loops on hook **(Fig 27)**.

One single crochet made. Work a single crochet (repeat Steps 1 and 2) in each remaining chain.

To work additional rows, chain 1 and turn work counterclockwise. Inserting hook under 2 top loops of the stitch **(Fig 28)**, work a single crochet (as before) in each stitch across.

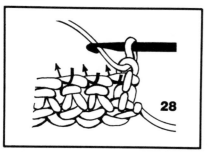

Double Crochet (dc)

Double crochet is a taller stitch than single crochet. Begin by making a chain to desired length.

Step 1: Bring yarn once over the hook; insert hook in the top loop of the 4th chain from hook **(Fig 29)**. Hook yarn and draw through **(Fig 30)**.

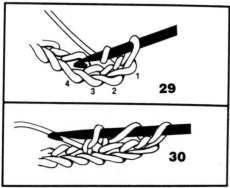

Step 2: Hook yarn and draw through first 2 loops on hook **(Fig 31)**.

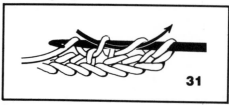

Step 3: Hook yarn and draw through last 2 loops on hook **(Fig 32)**.

One double crochet made. Work a double crochet (repeat Steps 1 through 3) in each remaining chain.

To work additional rows, make 3 chains and turn work counterclockwise. Beginning in 2nd stitch **(Fig 33—3** chains count as first double crochet), work a double crochet (as before) in each stitch across (remember to insert hook under 2 top loops of stitch). At end of row, work last double crochet in the top chain of chain-3 **(Fig 34)**.

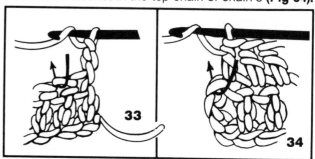

Half Double Crochet (hdc)

This stitch eliminates one step of double crochet—hence its name. It is taller than single crochet, but shorter than double crochet. Begin by making a chain to desired length.

Step 1: Bring yarn over hook; insert hook in top loop of 3rd chain from hook, hook yarn and draw through (3 loops now on hook).

Step 2: Hook yarn and draw through all 3 loops on hook **(Fig 35)**.

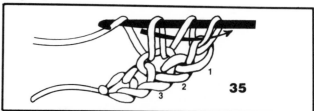

One half double crochet made. Work a half double crochet (repeat Steps 1 and 2) in each remaining chain.

To work additional rows, make 2 chains and turn work counterclockwise. Beginning in 2nd stitch (2 chains count as first half double crochet), work a half double crochet (as before) in each stitch across. At end of row, work last half double crochet in the top chain of chain-2.

Triple Crochet (tr)

Triple crochet is a tall stitch that works up quickly. First, make a chain to desired length.

Step 1: Bring yarn twice over the hook, insert hook in 5th chain from hook **(Fig 36)**; hook yarn and draw through **(Fig 37).**

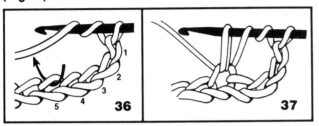

Step 2: Hook yarn and draw through first 2 loops on hook **(Fig 38).**

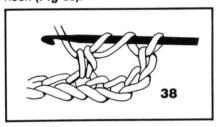

Step 3: Hook yarn and draw through next 2 loops on hook **(Fig 39).**

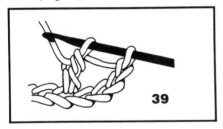

Step 4: Hook yarn and draw through remaining 2 loops on hook **(Fig 40).**

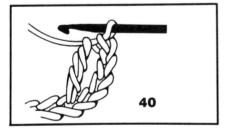

One triple crochet made. Work a triple crochet (repeat Steps 1 through 4) in each remaining chain.

To work additional rows, make 4 chains and turn work counterclockwise. Beginning in 2nd stitch (4 chains count as first triple crochet), work a double crochet (as before) in each stitch across. At end of row, work last triple crochet in the top chain of chain-4.

Slip Stitch (sl st)

This is the shortest of all crochet stitches, and usually is used to join work, or to move yarn across a group of stitches without adding height. To practice, make a chain to desired length; then work one row of double crochets.

Step 1: Insert hook in first st; hook yarn and draw through both stitch and loop on hook in one motion **(Fig 41).**

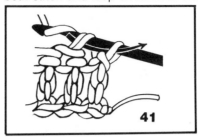

One slip stitch made. Work a slip stitch (repeat Step 1) in each stitch across.

FRINGE

Basic Instructions

Cut a piece of cardboard about 6″ wide and half as long as specified in instructions for strands plus ½″ for trimming allowance. Wind yarn loosely and evenly lengthwise around cardboard. When card is filled, cut yarn across one end. Do this several times, then begin fringing; you can wind additional strands as you need them.

Single Knot Fringe

Hold specified number of strands for one knot of fringe together, then fold in half. Hold afghan with right side facing you. Use crochet hook to draw folded end through space or stitch from right to wrong side **(Figs 42 and 43)**, pull loose ends through folded section **(Fig 44)** and draw knot up firmly **(Fig 45)**. Space knots as indicated in pattern instructions. Trim ends of fringe evenly.

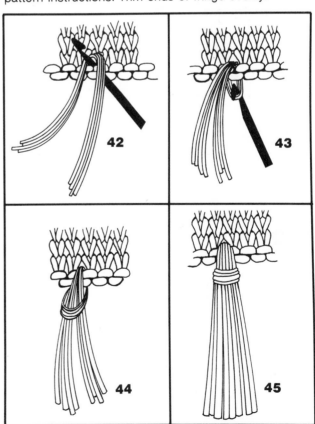

Double Knot Fringe

Begin by working Single Knot Fringe completely across one end of afghan. With right side facing you and working from left to right, take half the strands of one knot and half the strands in the knot next to it, and knot them together **(Fig 46)**.

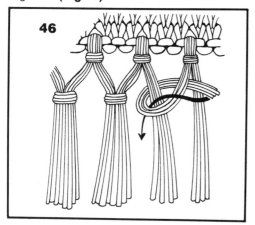

Triple Knot Fringe

First work Double Knot Fringe. Then working again on right side from left to right, tie third row of knots as in **Fig 47.**

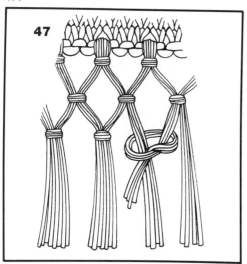

SYMBOLS

* An asterisk is used to mark the beginning of a portion of instructions which will be worked more than once; thus, ''rep from * twice'' means after working the instructions once, repeat the instructions following the asterisk twice more (3 times in all).

† The dagger identifies a portion of instructions that will be repeated again later in the pattern.

= The number after an equal sign at the end of a row indicates the number of stitches you should have when the row has been completed.

( ) Parentheses are used to enclose instructions which should be worked the exact number of times specified immediately following the parentheses, such as: (K1, P1) twice. They are also used to set off and clarify a group of sts that are to be worked all into the same sp or st, such as (2 dc, ch 1, 2 dc) in corner sp.

[ ] Brackets and ( ) parentheses are used to provide additional information to clarify instructions.

ABBREVIATIONS

Knit Abbreviations

BO	bind off
CO	cast on
dpn	double pointed needle
K	knit
P	purl
PSSO	pass slipped stitch over
stock st	stockinette stitch (knit 1 row, purl 1 row)

Crochet Abbreviations

ch(s)	chain(s)
dc	double crochet(s)
hdc	half double crochet(s)
sc	single crochet(s)
sl st(s)	slip stitch(es)
Tch	turning chain
tr	triple crochet(s)

Knit and Crochet Abbreviations

beg	begin(ning)
dec	decrease (-ing)
Fig	figure
inc	increase (-ing)
patt	pattern
prev	previous
rem	remain(ing)
rep	repeat(ing)
rnd(s)	round(s)
sk	skip
sl	slip
sp(s)	space(s)
st(s)	stitch(es)
tog	together
YO	yarn over

WORK EVEN This term in instructions means to continue working in the pattern as established, without increasing or decreasing.

Chapter 2

Easiest Afghans

knitted mohair
VICTORIAN LACE
designed by Jean Leinhauser

This traditional lace pattern has only a four-row repeat, and works up quickly on a large needle. Made with mohair yarn, it is light but warm.

SIZE: Approx 42″ x 64″

MATERIALS
Jaeger "Gabrielle" Mohair Yarn in 50 gm (1¾ oz) balls: 14 balls Hyacinth
Size 13, 36″ circular knitting needle (or size required for gauge)
Materials Note: For yarn source (C. J. Bates & Son), see page 4 .

GAUGE: In pattern stitch, 10 sts = 4″

INSTRUCTIONS
CO 105 sts *loosely.* Do not join; work back and forth in rows. Work in pattern stitch as follows.

Row 1 (wrong side): Purl.

Row 2: K2; * YO, sl 1, K1, PSSO; K1, K2 tog; YO, K1; rep from * across, ending last rep with K2 instead of K1. [**Note:** Each YO counts as one st throughout patt.]

Row 3: Purl.

Row 4: K3; * YO, sl 1, K2 tog, PSSO; YO, K3; rep from * across.

Rep Rows 1 through 4 until afghan measures approx 64″ from CO edge, ending by working Row 1. BO all sts *loosely* in knit. Weave in all ends.

knitted
LEMON LIME SHERBET

designed by Jean Leinhauser

Size: Approx 48″ x 63″ before fringing

MATERIALS
American Thread Dawn Sayelle* Knitting Worsted
Size Yarn: 4 skeins (4 oz each) White;
**   18 skeins (3 oz each) Lemon Lime**
Size 13, 29″ circular knitting needle (or size required for gauge)
Materials Note: Yarn is used doubled (2 strands of one color) throughout patt.

Gauge: With 2 strands of yarn in pattern stitch,
**   11 sts = 3″; 12 rows = 4″**

PATTERN STITCH
Row 1 (wrong side): Purl.

Row 2: K2 tog; * (K1, YO, K1) all in next st; sl 1 as to purl, K2 tog, PSSO; rep from * to last 3 sts; (K1, YO, K1) all in next st; sl 1 as to purl, K1, PSSO. [**Note:** Each YO counts as one st.]

Rep Rows 1 and 2 for patt.

INSTRUCTIONS
Note: Use 2 strands of yarn throughout patt.
With 2 strands of White, CO 177 sts *loosely*. Do not join; work back and forth in rows.

Border: Rep Rows 1 and 2 of Patt St in the following 14-row color sequence: 2 rows each White, Lemon Lime, White, Lemon Lime, White, Lemon Lime and White.

When 14 rows of border have been completed, use Lemon Lime only and work in Patt St until piece measures approx 60″ from CO edge, ending by working Row 2.

Border: Work same as other border.

BO all sts *loosely* in purl. Weave in all ends.

Fringe
Following *Fringe* instructions on page 9, make single knot fringe. Cut 14″ strands of White. Using 8 strands for each knot of fringe, tie 45 knots evenly spaced across each short end of afghan.

knitted
BURGUNDY
HONEYCOMB

designed by Jean Leinhauser

This easy afghan uses slip stitches to create the textured honeycomb effect.

SIZE: Approx 45″ x 62″

MATERIALS
Worsted weight yarn:
      16 oz burgundy;
      20 oz light pink/dark pink/burgundy ombre
Sizes 8 and 10½, 36″ circular knitting needles (or
  sizes required for gauge)

GAUGE: With smaller size needle in garter stitch,
        9 sts = 2″
     With larger size needle in pattern stitch,
        9 sts = 2″

INSTRUCTIONS
With burgundy and smaller size needle, CO 204 sts *loosely*. Do not join; work back and forth in rows. Knit 7 rows. Change to larger size needle and knit 2 more rows. Now work in pattern stitch as follows.

Color Notes: Pattern stitch is worked with 1 ball of ombre and 2 separate balls of burgundy (one at each end). On first row, join yarn as needed, leaving approx 4″ ends for weaving in later. On each following row, always pick up new yarn from underneath previous strand to prevent a hole in your work **(Fig 1)**.

Row 1 (right side): With burgundy, K5; with ombre, * YB (yarn to back of work), sl 2 as to purl (now and throughout patt), K6; rep from * to last 7 sts, sl 2; with 2nd ball of burgundy, K5.

Row 2: With burgundy, K5; with ombre, * YF (yarn to front of work), sl 2, P6; rep from * to last 7 sts, sl 2; with burgundy, K5.

Rows 3 through 6: Rep Rows 1 and 2, twice. At end of Row 6, drop ombre (do not cut).

Row 7: With burgundy, knit to last 5 sts; with other ball of burgundy, K5.

Row 8: With burgundy, K5; with other ball of burgundy, knit to end.

Row 9: With burgundy, K5; with ombre, K4, sl 2; * K6, YB, sl 2; rep from * to last 9 sts, K4; with burgundy, K5.

Row 10: With burgundy, K5; with ombre, YF, P4, sl 2; * P6, YF, sl 2; rep from * to last 9 sts, P4; with burgundy, K5.

Rows 11 through 14: Rep Rows 9 and 10, twice.

Rows 15 and 16: Rep Rows 7 and 8.

Rep Rows 1 through 16 until afghan measures approx 61″ from CO edge, ending by working Row 16. Change to smaller size needle. Continuing with burgundy (one ball only), knit 7 more rows. BO all sts *loosely* in knit. Weave in all ends. Steam lightly on wrong side.

crocheted
COLORADO STRIPES

designed by Jean Leinhauser

This one-row pattern stitch is quick and fun to work. We used rug yarn, but you can substitute worsted weight by changing hook size to achieve gauge.

SIZE: Approx 48″ x 66″

MATERIALS
Aunt Lydia's Heavy Rug Yarn in 70-yd skeins:
       12 skeins Natural;
       18 skeins Brick Heather
Size I aluminum crochet hook (or size required for gauge)

GAUGE: In pattern stitch,
    one sc + 3 chs = 1″; 3 rows = 1″

INSTRUCTIONS

With Brick Heather, ch 194 *loosely.* Work in pattern stitch as follows.

Row 1 (foundation row): Sc in 2nd ch from hook; * ch 3, sk 3 chs, sc in next ch; rep from * across.

Row 2 (patt row): Ch 1, turn; sc in first sc; * ch 3, sc in next sc; rep from * across.

Rows 3 through 5: Rep Row 2, 3 times. At end of Row 5, change to Natural in last sc. [**To Change Colors: Work sc until 2 lps rem on hook; cut color being used, leaving 4″ end for weaving in later. With new color (leave 4″ end), complete st (YO hook and pull through 2 lps on hook) = color changed.**]

Rep Row 2 in the following 12-row color sequence:
    2 rows Natural
    1 row Brick Heather
    1 row Natural
    1 row Brick Heather
    2 rows Natural
    5 rows Brick Heather

Rep 12-row color sequence, 15 times more. Finish off; weave in all ends securely.

crocheted
PERSIMMON

designed by Eleanor Denner

SIZE: Approx 45″ x 60″

MATERIALS
Worsted weight yarn: 4 oz light persimmon;
24 oz medium persimmon;
8 oz dark persimmon
Size I aluminum crochet hook (or size required for gauge)

GAUGE: In sc, 7 sts = 2″

INSTRUCTIONS

With dk persimmon, ch 159 *loosely.*

Row 1 (foundation row): Sc in 2nd ch from hook and in each rem ch across = 158 sc.

Row 2 (patt row): Ch 3, turn; dc dec over next 2 sc [**To Make Dc Dec: (YO, insert hook in next sc and draw up a lp—Fig 1; YO and draw through 2 lps on hook) twice (3 lps now on hook — Fig 2); YO and draw through all 3 lps on hook (Fig 3) = dc dec made.**] * ch 1, dc dec over next 2 sc; rep from * to last sc, dc in last sc.

Row 3 (patt row): Ch 1, turn; sc in each of first 2 sts; * sc in ch-1 sp, sc in next st; rep from * across, ending sc in sp under turning ch, sc in 2nd ch of ch-3 = 158 sc.

Rep Rows 2 and 3 in the following color sequence for border, changing colors as needed [**To Change Colors: Finish off color being used at end of row, leaving 4″ end for weaving in later. Join new color (leave 4″ end) with a sl st in top of last st of row; then continue with next row.**]:

> 2 rows dk persimmon
> 4 rows lt persimmon
> 2 rows dk persimmon
> 4 rows lt persimmon
> 4 rows dk persimmon

When last row of border is completed, finish off dk persimmon. You should now have 19 rows total.

Continuing with med persimmon only, work in pattern stitch (rep Rows 2 and 3) until work measures approx 52″ long, ending by working Row 2. Finish off med persimmon; then work border as follows.

Continuing in pattern stitch (beg with Row 3), work color sequence of other border in reverse, ending by working 5 rows of dk persimmon. Finish off; weave in all ends.

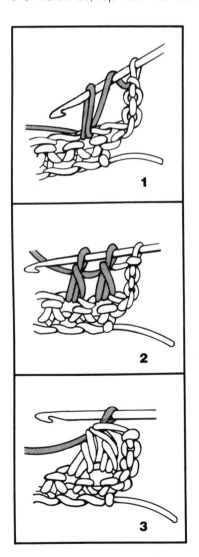

crocheted
BLUE SKIES

designed by Mary Thomas

SIZE: Approx 46″ x 68″ before fringing

MATERIALS
Worsted weight yarn: 38 oz powder blue
Size J aluminum crochet hook (or size required for gauge)

GAUGE: In dc, 10 sts = 3½″

INSTRUCTIONS
Ch 133 *loosely*.

Row 1: Dc in 4th ch from hook and in each rem ch across = 131 dc (counting beg ch-3).

Row 2: Ch 3, turn; sk next dc, tr (see instructions on page 9) in each of next 2 dc, tr in skipped dc **(Fig 1)**; * sk next

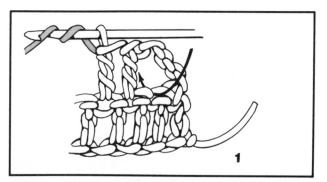

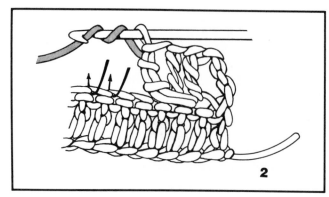

dc, tr in each of next 2 dc **(Fig 2)**, tr in skipped dc; rep from * across, ending tr in top of ch-3.

Row 3: Ch 3, turn; dc in next tr and in each tr across, ending dc in top of ch-3 = 131 dc (counting beg ch-3).

Row 4: Ch 3, turn; tr in next dc and in each dc across, ending tr in top of ch-3.

Row 5: Rep Row 3.

Rep Rows 2 through 5 until afghan measures approx 68″ long, ending by working Row 3. Finish off; weave in all ends.

Fringe
Following *Fringe* instructions on page 9, make single knot fringe. Cut 24″ strands of yarn; use 4 strands for each knot of fringe. Working across each short end of afghan, tie one knot in sp between 2 sts at each end; then tie rem knots in sps between sts, having 3 sts between each knot of fringe.

crocheted
GRANNY RIPPLE

designed by Joan Kokaska

This pattern combines two favorites: the ripple design with the granny-type 3-dc groups.

SIZE: Approx 46″ x 70″

MATERIALS
Worsted weight yarn: 26 oz bright navy;
14 oz red;
14 oz light beige
Size I aluminum crochet hook (or size required for gauge)

GAUGE: In dc, 13 sts = 4″

INSTRUCTIONS

With navy, ch 210 *loosely.*

Row 1: Sc in 2nd ch from hook and in each rem ch across = 209 sc.

Row 2: Ch 3, turn; sk first 3 sc, (3 dc in next sc, sk 2 sc) 3 times; work (3 dc, ch 3, 3 dc) in next sc for point; * (sk 2 sc, 3 dc in next sc) twice; sk 2 sc, cluster in next sc [**To Work Cluster: (YO, insert hook in st and draw up a lp; YO and draw through 2 lps on hook) 3 times (Fig 1); YO and draw through all 4 lps on hook = cluster made.**]; sk 4 sc, cluster in next sc; (sk 2 sc, 3 dc in next sc) twice; sk 2 sc, work (3 dc, ch 3, 3 dc) in next sc for point; rep from * 7 times more; sk 2 sc, (3 dc in next sc, sk 2 sc) 3 times, dc in last sc.

Row 3 (patt row): Ch 3, turn; sk first sp (between first dc and 3-dc group); work 3 dc in each of next 3 sps (between each pair of 3-dc groups); (3 dc, ch 3, 3 dc) in ch-3 sp at point; * work 3 dc in each of next 2 sps; cluster in next sp, sk sp between clusters, cluster in next sp; work 3 dc in each of next 2 sps, (3 dc, ch 3, 3 dc) in ch-3 sp at point; rep from * 7 times more; work 3 dc in each of next 3 sps, dc in last sp (between last 3-dc group and ch-3).

Rows 4 through 7: Rep Row 3, four times. At end of Row 7, change to red in last dc. [**To Change Colors: Work dc until 2 lps rem on hook; finish off color being used, leaving 4″ end for weaving in later. With new color (leave 4″ end), YO and draw through 2 lps on hook = color changed.**]

Rep Row 3 in the following 12-row color sequence:
    3 rows red
    3 rows beige
    6 rows navy

Rep 12-row color sequence, 7 times more. At end of last row, finish off. Weave in all ends.

Rows 2 through 4: Ch 1, turn; sc in each sc across. At end of Row 4, drop white; do not cut (white is carried up along side of work).

Row 5 (rainbow color row): With purple (leave approx 4″ end), ch 1, turn; working over yarn end [**To Work Over Yarn End: Place end on top of row and work beg sts over it — Fig 1.**], sc in each sc across.

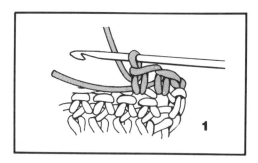

Row 6 (rainbow ripple row): Ch 3, turn; sl st around post (from front to back to front) of 2nd sc in 5th row below **(Fig 2),** ch 3. Return to working row; sk first 2 sc, * sl st around post of next sc, ch 3. Working in 5th row below, sk one sc (from where prev sl st was worked); sl st around post of next sc, ch 3. Return to working row; sk next sc; rep from * to last sc, sl st in last sc (do not work st around post). Cut yarn, leaving 4″ end.

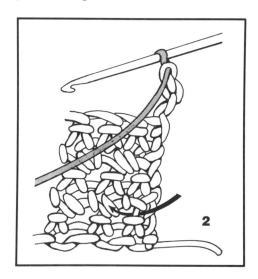

Row 7: With white, ch 1, turn; working over yarn end (as before), sc in each sc across.

Rows 8 through 55: Rep Rows 2 through 7, eight times more, using the following rainbow color sequence for Rows 5 and 6 of each repeat:

blue
turquoise
med green
lime green
yellow
lt orange
dk orange
red

Rep Rows 2 through 55 (complete rainbow color sequence), 4 times more. Finish off; weave in yarn ends.

crocheted
RAINBOW RIPPLE
designed by Joan Kokaska

This is the most colorful afghan we've ever seen — and one of the most delightful to make. Try it as a bedspread on a child's bed; or, create a completely different look by working the afghan in two colors only: cream for the background and brown for the color rows, for example.

SIZE: Approx 46″ x 62″

MATERIALS
Worsted weight yarn:
   Main color: 32 oz white;
   Rainbow colors: 3½ oz each purple, medium blue, turquoise, medium green, bright lime green, bright yellow, light orange, dark orange and red
Size J aluminum crochet hook (or size required for gauge)

GAUGE: In sc, 3 sts = 1″

INSTRUCTIONS
With white, ch 139 *loosely.*

Row 1 (wrong side): Sc in 2nd ch from hook and in each rem ch across = 138 sc.

knitted mohair
CRISS CROSS

designed by Mary Thomas

SIZE: Approx 48″ x 68″

MATERIALS
Jaeger "Gabrielle" Mohair Yarn in 50 gm (1¾ oz)
   balls: 16 balls Mulberry
Size 15, 36″ circular knitting needle (or size required
   for gauge)
Materials Note: For yarn source (C. J. Bates & Son),
see page 4 .

GAUGE: In garter st, 5 sts = 2″

INSTRUCTIONS
CO 120 sts *loosely*. Do not join; work back and forth in
rows. Knit first 4 rows; then work in patt as follows.

Row 1: K4; * K1 with 3 wraps [**To Work K1 with 3 Wraps:
Insert needle into next st as if to knit, wrap yarn 3
times around tip of right-hand needle; then knit this
st, carrying extra wraps on right-hand needle (Fig 1)
= K1 with 3 wraps.**]; rep from * to last 4 sts, K4.

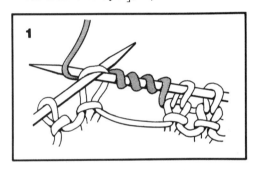

Row 2 (right side): K4; * work Criss-Cross st over next 8
sts [**To Work Criss-Cross st: (Sl next st to right-hand
needle as to purl, dropping extra wraps) 8 times (Fig
2); with left-hand needle, sk first 4 sl sts on right-hand
needle and insert through next 4 sl sts (Fig 3); pull
these 4 sl sts over the 4 skipped sl sts, being careful
not to twist sts (Fig 4); now sl the 4 skipped sl sts back
onto left-hand needle; then knit these 8 sts, being
careful not to twist the sts = Criss-Cross st made.**];
rep from * to last 4 sts, K4.

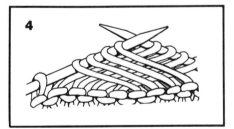

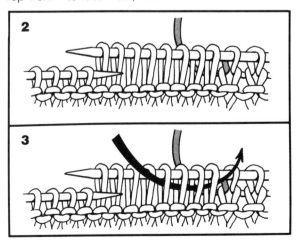

Rows 3, 4, 5 and 6: Knit.

Row 7: K8; * K1 with 3 wraps; rep from * to last 8 sts, K8.

Row 8: K8; * work Criss-Cross st over next 8 sts; rep from *
to last 8 sts, K8.

Rows 9, 10, 11 and 12: Knit.

Rep Rows 1 through 12 until work measures approx 66″
from CO edge; then rep Rows 1 through 6 once more. BO
all sts *loosely* in knit. Weave in all ends.

crocheted
KITTENS

designed by Joan Kokaska

Kittens in a row cheerfully peer out from this unusual afghan, which works up quickly and is fun to make.

Size: Approx 40″ x 60″ before fringing

MATERIALS
Worsted weight yarn: 16 oz gray;
16 oz black;
22 oz white
Size H aluminum crochet hook (or size required for gauge)

GAUGE: 4 Shells = 5″

INSTRUCTIONS

With black, ch 164 *loosely.*

Row 1: Dc in 4th ch from hook and in next ch; sk 2 chs, 2 dc in next ch; ch 1, 2 dc in next ch; * sk 3 chs, 2 dc in next ch; ch 1, 2 dc in next ch; rep from * to last 5 chs; sk 2 chs, dc in each of last 3 chs.

Row 2: Ch 3, turn; dc in each of next 2 dc, sk next 2 dc, work a shell (2 dc, ch 1, 2 dc) in next ch-1 sp; * sk next 4 dc, work a shell in next ch-1 sp; rep from * to last 4 dc; sk next 2 dc, dc in each of next 2 dc; dc in top of ch-3, changing to white. [**To Change Colors: Work dc until 2 lps rem on hook; finish off color being used, leaving approx 4″ end for weaving in later. With new color (leave 4″ end), YO and draw through 2 lps on hook = color changed.**]

Row 3: With white, ch 3, turn; dc in each of next 2 dc; * work a shell in ch-1 sp of next shell; work a puff st between shells in 2nd row below [**To Work Puff St: (YO and insert hook between shells in 2nd row below — Fig 1; hook yarn and draw up a long lp to height of working row) 4 times (9 lps now on hook — Fig 2); YO and draw through 8 lps on hook, then YO and draw through 2 rem lps on hook = puff st made.**]; rep from * to last shell; work a shell in ch-1 sp of last shell, dc in each of next 2 dc, dc in top of ch-3.

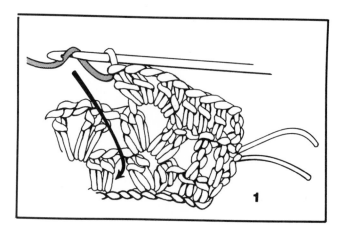

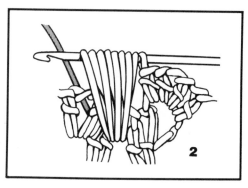

Row 4: Ch 3, turn; dc in each of next 2 dc, * work a shell in ch-1 sp of next shell; rep from * to last 2 dc; dc in each of last 2 dc, dc in top of ch-3.

Row 5: Rep Row 4, changing to gray at end of row (as before).

Rows 6 through 8: With gray, rep Rows 3 through 5. At end of Row 8, change to black.

Rows 9 through 11: With black, rep Rows 3 through 5. At end of Row 11, change to white.

Rep Rows 3 through 11 until afghan measures approx 60″ long, ending by working Row 10 (2 rows of black completed). Finish off; weave in all ends.

Fringe
Following *Fringe* instructions on page 9, make single knot fringe. Cut 14″ strands of white; use 12 strands for each knot of fringe. Working across each short end of afghan, tie one knot in each sp between shells and in sp at each end (between dc and shell).

Chapter 3

Great Classics

crocheted
SPRINGTIME RIPPLE
designed by Mary Thomas

SIZE: Approx 48″ x 70″

MATERIALS
Worsted weight yarn: 6 oz light green;
12 oz medium green;
12 oz dark green;
24 oz white
Size J aluminum crochet hook (or size required for gauge)

GAUGE: In sc, 3 sts = 1″; 7 rows = 2″

INSTRUCTIONS

With dk green, ch 210 *loosely*.

Row 1 (foundation row): Sc in 2nd ch from hook and in each of next 4 chs, 3 sc in next ch; * sc in each of next 3 chs, sk 2 chs; sc in each of next 3 chs, 3 sc in next ch; rep from * to last 5 chs, sc in each of rem 5 chs.

Row 2 (right side): Ch 1, turn; **working in back lp only (lp away from you — Fig 1) of each st across,** dec over first 2 sts [**To Work Dec: Draw up a lp in each of the next 2 sts, YO and draw through all 3 lps on hook = dec made.**]; sc in each of next 4 sts, 3 sc in next st; * sc in each of next 3 sts, sk 2 sts; sc in each of next 3 sts, 3 sc in next st; rep from * to last 6 sts; sc in each of next 4 sts, dec over last 2 sts.

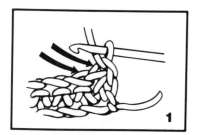

Rows 3 through 5: Rep Row 2, three times. At end of Row 5, leaving 4″ ends for weaving in later, finish off dk green; join lt green with a sl st **in front lp only** (lp toward you) of last st worked.

Row 6: With lt green, ch 1, turn; sl st LOOSELY **in both lps** of each sc across. At end of row, leaving 4″ ends, finish off lt green; join white with a sl st **in front lp only** of sc where last sl st was worked.

Note: At beg of next row, work over yarn ends for several sts as shown in **Fig 2.**

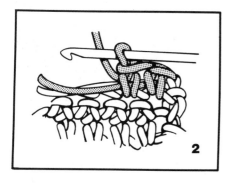

Row 7: Continuing with white, ch 1, turn; working **in back lp only** of each sc across (leave sl sts unworked), rep Row 2.

Row 8: Ch 1, turn; working **in both lps** of each sc across, dec over first 2 sc, sc in each of next 4 sc; work (BB [*blackberry st*], sc, BB) all in next sc [**To Work BB: Insert hook in st and draw up a lp, (YO and draw**

through last lp on hook) 3 times; YO and draw through both lps on hook (Fig 3), keeping ch-3 just made to front of work = BB made.]; * sc in each of next 3 sc, sk 2 sc; sc in each of next 3 sc, work (BB, sc, BB) all in next sc; rep from * to last 6 sc; sc in each of next 4 sc, dec over last 2 sc.

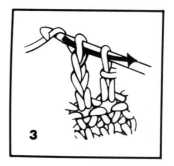

Row 9: Working **in both lps** of each st across (instead of back lp only), rep Row 2.

Row 10: Ch 1, turn; working **in both lps** of each sc across, dec over first 2 sc, sc in each of next 2 sc; BB in next sc, sc in next sc; work (BB, sc, BB) all in next sc; * sc in next sc, BB in next sc; sc in next sc, sk 2 sc, sc in next sc; BB in next sc, sc in next sc; work (BB, sc, BB) all in next sc; rep from * to last 6 sc; sc in next sc, BB in next sc; sc in each of next 2 sc, dec over last 2 sc.

Row 11: Rep Row 9. At end of row, leaving 4″ ends for weaving in later, finish off white; join lt green with a sl st **in front lp only** of last st worked.

Row 12: Rep Row 6. At end of row, finish off lt green; join med green (instead of white).

Row 13: Continuing with med green and working over yarn ends, rep Row 7.

Rows 14 through 17: With med green; rep Row 2, four times. At end of Row 17, leaving 4″ ends for weaving in later, finish off med green; join lt green with a sl st in front lp only of last st worked.

Rows 18 through 24: Rep Rows 6 through 12. At end of Row 24, finish off lt green; join dk green.

Row 25: Continuing with dk green, rep Row 7.

Rep Rows 2 through 25, seven times more; then rep Rows 2 through 5 once. Finish off; weave in all yarn ends.

crocheted ripple
FALL LEAVES
designed by Jean Leinhauser

SIZE: Approx 42″ x 62″

MATERIALS
Worsted weight yarn: 24 oz dark rust;
12 oz burnt orange;
8 oz ecru
Size J aluminum crochet hook (or size required for gauge)

GAUGE: In sc, 3 sts = 1″

INSTRUCTIONS
With rust, ch 167 *loosely.*

Row 1 (foundation row): Sc in 2nd ch from hook, sk one ch, sc in each of next 4 chs; * 3 sc in next ch, sc in each of next 3 chs; sk 2 chs, sc in each of next 3 chs; rep from * to last 7 chs; 3 sc in next ch, sc in each of next 4 chs; sk one ch, sc in last ch.

Row 2 (wrong side): Ch 1, turn; sc in first sc, sk one sc, sc in each of next 4 sc; * 3 sc in next sc, sc in each of next 3 sc; sk 2 sc, sc in each of next 3 sc; rep from * to last 7 sc; 3 sc in next sc, sc in each of next 4 sc; sk one sc, sc in last sc.

Row 3: Rep Row 2, changing to orange in last st. [**To Change Colors: Work last st until 2 lps rem on hook; cut old color, leaving 4″ end. With new color (leave 4″ end), complete st (YO and draw through both lps on hook) = color changed.**]

Note: At beg of next row and on following rows after a color change, work over yarn ends for several sts as shown in **Fig 1**.

Rows 4 and 5: With orange, rep Row 2, twice. At end of Row 5, change to ecru in last st.

Row 6: With ecru, rep Row 2, changing to rust in last st.

Row 7 (PC row): With rust, ch 2, turn; sk first sc, dc in each of next 3 sc, PC (popcorn) in next sc [**To Make PC: Work 4 dc in st; remove hook from lp and insert in first dc of 4-dc group just made (Fig 2); then hook dropped lp and pull through lp on hook, ch 1 = PC made.**]; dc in next sc, 3 dc in next sc; * dc in next sc, PC in next sc; work cluster over next 4 sc [**To Work Cluster: (YO, insert hook in next sc and draw up a lp, YO and draw through 2 lps on hook) 4 times (Fig 3); YO and draw through all 5 lps on hook = cluster made.**]; PC in next sc, dc in next sc, 3 dc in next sc; rep from * to last 6 sc; dc in next sc, PC in next sc, dc in each of next 2 sc; work dc dec over last 2 sc, changing to ecru as follows: (YO, insert hook in next sc and draw up a lp, YO and draw through 2 lps on hook) twice; cut rust. With ecru, YO and draw through all 3 lps on hook.

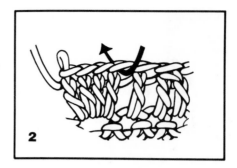

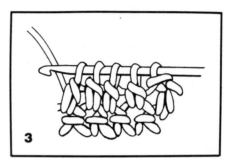

Row 8: With ecru, ch 1, turn; sc in first st (dc dec), sk next dc; sc in next dc, sc in PC (work in dc where dropped lp was pulled through); sc in each of next 2 dc, 3 sc in next dc, sc in each of next 2 dc; * sc in PC, sk cluster, sc in next PC; sc in each of next 2 dc, 3 sc in next dc, sc in each of next 2 dc; rep from * to last PC; sc in PC, sc in next dc, sk next dc; sc in last dc, changing to orange.

Rows 9 and 10: With orange, rep Row 2, twice. At end of Row 10, change to rust in last st.

Row 11: With rust, Rep Row 2.

Rep Rows 2 through 11 until work measures approx 62″ long. Continuing with rust, rep Row 2, twice more. Finish off; weave in all ends. Lightly steam press edges on wrong side to prevent curling.

crocheted
CONTEMPORARY GRANNY
designed by Carol Wilson Mansfield

SIZE: Approx 52″ x 64″

MATERIALS
Worsted weight yarn: 24 oz white;
10 oz medium blue;
12 oz light gray;
18 oz dark gray;
6 oz black
Size H aluminum crochet hook (or size required for gauge)

GAUGE: One granny square (6 rnds) = 6″

GRANNY SQUARE INSTRUCTIONS
[**Note:** *All rnds are worked on right side.*]

With color specified for first rnd, leaving a 3″ yarn end, ch 4; join with a sl st to form a ring.

Rnd 1: Continuing with same color, ch 3; working over 3″ yarn end, 2 dc in ring; (ch 2, 3 dc in ring) 3 times, ch 2; join with a sl st in top of beg ch-3. Finish off, leaving 3″ yarn end for weaving in now or when square is completed.

Rnd 2: Do not turn; join 2nd color with a sl st in any ch-2 sp; ch 3, (2 dc, ch 2, 3 dc) in same sp as joining [first corner made]; * (3 dc, ch 2, 3 dc) in next ch-2 sp [corner made]; rep from * twice more; join with a sl st in top of beg ch-3. Finish off in same manner as prev rnd.

Rnd 3: Do not turn; join 3rd color with a sl st in any ch-2 corner sp; ch 3, (2 dc, ch 2, 3 dc) in same sp as joining; * 3 dc between next two 3-dc groups for side, (3 dc, ch 2, 3 dc) in next corner sp; rep from * twice more, 3 dc between next two 3-dc groups for last side; join with a sl st in top of beg ch-3. Do not finish off.

Rnd 4: Do not turn; continuing with color of prev rnd, sl st in each of next 2 dc and into corner sp; † ch 3, (2 dc, ch 2, 3 dc) in same sp; * 3 dc between each pair of 3-dc groups along side, (3 dc, ch 2, 3 dc) in next corner sp; rep from * twice more, 3 dc between each pair of 3-dc groups along last side; join with a sl st in top of beg ch-3. Finish off. †

Rnd 5: Do not turn; join specified color with a sl st in any corner sp; work instructions in Rnd 4 from † to †.

Rnd 6: Rep Rnd 5. Weave in all ends.

AFGHAN INSTRUCTIONS

Following prev *Granny Square Instructions,* make a total of 63 squares as follows:

	Square A (make 18)	Square B (make 17)	Square C (make 28)
Rnd 1:	white	black	lt gray
Rnd 2:	black	lt gray	dk gray
Rnds 3 and 4:	lt gray	blue	white
Rnd 5:	blue	white	white*
Rnd 6:	dk gray	dk gray	white*

For Rnds 5 and 6 of Square C, continue with white and work in same manner as Rnd 4.

Assembling

Arrange squares as shown in **Fig 1**. To join, hold two squares with right sides tog. Thread matching yarn into tapestry needle. Carefully matching sts on both squares, sew with overcast st **in outer lps only (Fig 2)** across side, beg and ending with one corner st. Join squares in rows; then sew rows tog in same manner, being sure that all four-corner junctions are firmly joined.

C	C	C	C	C	C	C
C	A	B	A	B	A	C
C	B	A	B	A	B	C
C	A	B	A	B	A	C
C	B	A	B	A	B	C
C	A	B	A	B	A	C
C	B	A	B	A	B	C
C	A	B	A	B	A	C
C	C	C	C	C	C	C

1

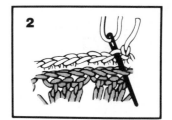

2

Edging

With right side facing, join dk gray with a sl st in any outer corner sp of afghan.

Rnd 1: Ch 3, (2 dc, ch 2, 3 dc) in same sp as joining; along each side edge of afghan, work 3 dc between each pair of 3-dc groups and in each corner sp of squares (on each side of joinings); and in each rem corner sp of afghan, work (3 dc, ch 2, 3 dc); join with a sl st in top of beg ch-3. Finish off.

Continue by working each rnd on right side in same manner as squares [3 dc between each pair of 3-dc groups along sides and (3 dc, ch 2, 3 dc) in each corner sp] in the following color sequence:

    1 rnd black

    3 rnds white

    2 rnds lt gray

    1 rnd blue

    3 rnds dk gray

When 11 rnds of edging have been completed, finish off and weave in all loose yarn ends.

Fisherman crochet
IRISH MIST

designed by Mary Thomas

For the crocheter — fascinating Aran stitches combined into a 5-panel afghan, surely to bring beauty and pleasure to your work.

SIZE: Approx 45″ x 66″ before fringing

MATERIALS
Worsted weight yarn: 60 oz ecru
Sizes J and K aluminum crochet hooks (or size required for gauge)

**GAUGE: With smaller size hook in each patt st,
3 sts = 1″**

SPECIAL NOTE: Before starting your afghan, we suggest practicing the Fisherman Pattern Stitches. Work several repeats of each pattern until you become familiar with the stitch and can obtain gauge (3 sts = 1″).

FISHERMAN PATTERN STITCHES

[**Note:** *Use smaller size hook for working each patt st.*]

CABLE (worked over 2 sts).
Rows 1, 2, 3 and 4: Sc in each sc across.
Row 5 (cable row): Sc in next sc; work cable [**To Work Cable: Ch 4, sl st around post of sc 4 rows below sc just made (Fig 1); turn work slightly so wrong side of ch-4 is facing you; sc in top lp only in each of the 4 chs (Fig 2) = cable made.**]; return to working row, sc in next sc (behind cable).

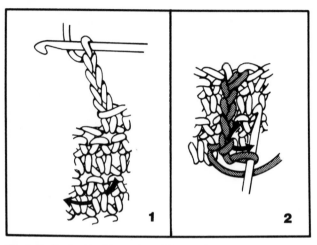

Row 6: Sc in next sc, sk cable, sc in next sc.

Rep Rows 3 through 6 for patt. [**Note:** *On each following cable row (Row 5), work sl st (following ch-4) around post of first sc in prev cable row* **(Fig 3).**]

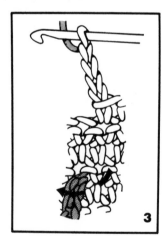

FRONT POST (worked over one st)
Rows 1 and 2: Sc in next sc.
Row 3: Work FP (front post) around post of next sc in 2nd row below **(Fig 4)** [**To Work FP: YO, insert hook around st from front to back to front; YO and draw lp through (3 lps now on hook); then complete st as a regular dc — (YO and draw through 2 lps on hook) twice = FP made.**]; return to working row, sk sc behind FP just made.

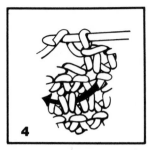

Row 4: Sc in top of FP.
Row 5: Work FP around post of FP in 2nd row below.

Rep Rows 4 and 5 for patt.

DIAMOND (worked over 9 sts)
Row 1: Sc each of next 4 sc ch 1 LOOSELY (now and throughout Diamond Patt); sk one sc, sc in each of next 4 sc.
Row 2: Sc in each of next 3 sc; ch 1, sk one sc, sc in ch-1 sp; ch 1, sk one sc, sc in each of next 3 sc.
Row 3: Sc in each of next 3 sc; (ch 1, sk ch-1 sp, sc in next sc) twice; sc in each of next 2 sc.
Row 4: Sc in each of next 2 sc; ch 1, sk one sc, sc in ch-1 sp; sc in next sc, sc in ch-1 sp; ch 1, sk one sc, sc in each of next 2 sc.
Row 5: Sc in each of next 2 sc; ch 1, sk ch-1 sp, sc in each of next 3 sc; ch 1, sk ch-1 sp, sc in each of next 2 sc.
Row 6 (PC row): Sc in next sc; ch 1, sk one sc, sc in ch-1 sp; sc in next sc, PC (popcorn) in next sc [**To Work PC: Work 5 sc in st; remove hook and insert hook in first sc of 5-sc group just made; hook dropped lp (Fig 5) and pull through st, ch 1 = PC made.**]; sc in next sc, sc in ch-1 sp; ch 1, sk one sc, sc in next sc.

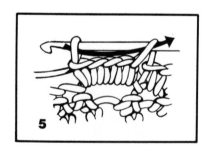

Row 7: Sc in next sc; ch 1, sk ch-1 sp, sc in each of next 2 sc; sc in PC (work in sc where dropped lp was pulled through), sc in each of next 2 sc; ch 1, sk ch-1 sp, sc in next sc.
Row 8: Sc in next sc, sc in ch-1 sp; ch 1, sk one sc, sc in each of next 3 sc; ch 1, sk one sc, sc in ch-1 sp, sc in next sc.
Row 9: Rep Row 5.
Row 10: Sc in each of next 2 sc, sc in ch-1 sp; ch 1, sk one sc, sc in next sc; ch 1, sk one sc, sc in ch-1 sp, sc in each of next 2 sc.
Row 11: Rep Row 3.
Row 12: Sc in each of next 3 sc, sc in ch-1 sp; ch 1, sk one sc, sc in ch-1 sp, sc in each of next 3 sc. [**Note:** *Your work should now resemble graph in* **Fig 6.**]

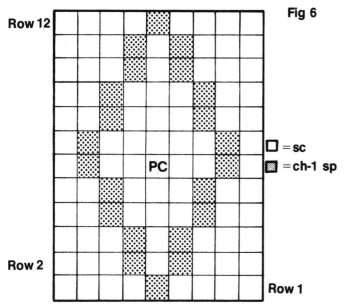

Fig 6

Row 12

Row 2

Row 1

PC

☐ = sc
▨ = ch-1 sp

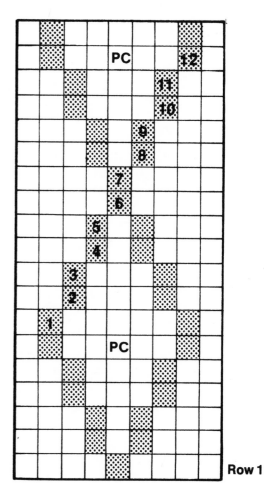

Fig 8

PC

12
11
10
9
8
7
6
5
4
3
2
1

PC

Row 1

Row 13: Sc in each of next 4 sc, ch 1, sk ch-1 sp, sc in each of next 4 sc.

Rep Rows 2 through 13 for patt. When all patt repeats are completed, work outline of diamonds as follows:

DIAMOND OUTLINE

⌈**Note:** *Outline is worked on right side, using larger size hook and 2 strands of yarn (yarn is held at back of work).*⌉

First Half: Insert larger size hook in ch-1 sp at bottom of first diamond patt (at beg edge) from front to back, hook 2 strands of yarn and pull up a lp, leaving 4″ ends for weaving in later. Working diagonally to the left, sl st in each of next 5 ch-1 sps (see **Fig 7**) ⌈**To Work Sl St: Insert hook in ch-1 sp, hook yarn from beneath work and draw through work and lp on hook = sl st made.**⌉; sl st in next ch-1 sp (above prev sl st). Now working diagonally to the right, sl st in each of next 12 sps **(Fig 8).** Continue working in this manner (diagonally to the left and then to the right) through all rows of Diamond Patt. Finish off; weave in all ends. Then work Second Half as follows.

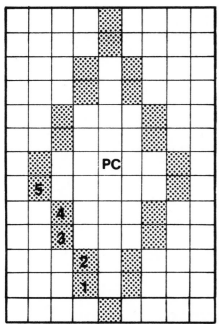

Fig 7

PC

5
4
3
2
1

Row 1

Second Half: Reversing direction (diagonally to the right and then diagonally to the left, etc.), work in same manner as First Half. ⌈**Note:** *On Rows 12 and 13 of each diamond repeat, you will be working into same ch-1 sps where sl sts were worked in First Half of outline (crossing over prev sl sts).*⌉

BLACKBERRY (worked over an uneven number of sts)
Row 1: Sc in each st across.
Row 2 (BB row): Sc in first sc; * BB (blackberry st) in next sc ⌈**To Work BB: Insert hook in st and draw up a lp; (YO and draw through last lp on hook) 3 times; YO and draw through both lps on hook (Fig 9), keeping ch-3 to front of work = BB made.**⌉, sc in next sc; rep from * across.

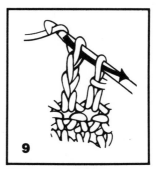

9

Row 3: Rep Row 1.
Row 4 (BB row): Sc in each of first 2 sc; * BB in next sc, sc in next sc; rep from * to last sc, sc in last sc.

Rep Rows 1 through 4 for patt. ⌈**Note:** *Blackberry sts will be alternating every other row.*⌉

29

AFGHAN INSTRUCTIONS

Panel A (make 3)
With smaller size hook, ch 30 *loosely.*

Row 1 (right side): Sc in 2nd ch from hook and in each rem ch across = 29 sc.

Row 2: Ch 1, turn; sc in each of first 10 sc, work Row 1 of Diamond Patt over next 9 sc; sc in each of last 10 sc.

Row 3: Ch 1, turn; sc in first sc; * **work (Row 3 of FP Patt) twice, sc in each of next 2 sc [remember to sk one sc behind each FP]; work Row 3 of FP Patt once [you will be skipping 2 sc from last FP in 2nd row below], sc in each of next 2 sc; work (Row 3 of FP patt) twice *;** work Row 2 of Diamond Patt; rep from * to * once; sc in last sc.

Row 4: Ch 1, turn; sc in each of first 10 sts, work Row 3 of Diamond Patt; sc in each of last 10 sts.

Row 5: Ch 1, turn; sc in first sc, * **work (Row 5 of FP Patt) twice, work Row 5 of Cable Patt over next 2 sts; work Row 5 of FP Patt once, work Row 5 of Cable Patt over next 2 sts; work (Row 5 of FP Patt) twice *;** work Row 4 of Diamond Patt; rep from * to * once; sc in last sc.

Row 6: Ch 1, turn; sc in each of first 4 sts, (sk cable, sc in each of next 3 sts) twice; work Row 5 of Diamond Patt; (sc in each of next 3 sts, sk cable) twice; sc in each of last 4 sts.

Row 7: Ch 1, turn; sc in first sc; * **work (Row 5 of FP Patt) twice, sc in each of next 2 sc; work (Row 5 of FP Patt) once, sc in each of next 2 sc; work (Row 5 of FP Patt) twice *;** work Row 6 of Diamond Patt; rep from * to * once; sc in last sc.

Row 8: Ch 1, turn; sc in each of first 10 sts, work Row 7 of Diamond Patt; sc in each of last 10 sts.

Row 9: Ch 1, turn; sc in first sc; rep from * to * in Row 5 of Panel A, once; work Row 8 of Diamond Patt; rep from * to * in Row 5 of Panel A, once; sc in last sc.

Row 10: Rep Row 6.

Row 11: Ch 1, turn; sc in first sc, rep from * to * in Row 7 of Panel A, once; work Row 10 of Diamond Patt; rep from * to * in Row 7 of Panel A, once; sc in last sc.

Row 12: Rep Row 4.

Row 13: Ch 1, turn; sc in first sc; rep from * to * in Row 5 of Panel A, once; work Row 12 of Diamond Patt; rep from * to * in Row 5 of Panel A, once; sc in last sc.

Row 14: Ch 1, turn; sc in each of first 4 sts, (sk cable, sc in each of next 3 sts) twice; work Row 13 of Diamond Patt; (sc in each of next 3 sts, sk cable) twice; sc in each of last 4 sts.

Row 15: Ch 1, turn; sc in first sc, rep from * to * in Row 7 of Panel A, once; work Row 2 of Diamond Patt; rep from * to * in Row 7 of Panel A, once; sc in last sc.

Rep Rows 4 through 15 until work measures approx 66" long, ending by working Row 13.

Last Row (wrong side): Ch 1, turn; sc in each of first 4 sts, (sk cable, sc in each of next 3 sts) twice; sc in each of next 4 sc, sc in ch-1 sp, sc in each of next 7 sts; (sk cable, sc in each of next 3 sts) twice, sc in last sc. Finish off.

Work Diamond Outline (follow instructions on page 29) on center diamond patt. Weave in all ends.

Panel B (make 2)
With smaller size hook, ch 26 *loosely.*

Row 1 (wrong side): Sc in 2nd ch from hook and in each rem ch across = 25 sc.

Note: At beg of each following row, ch 1 and turn.

Following instructions for Blackberry Pattern, beg with Row 2 and work in patt until panel measures same length as Panel A, ending by working Row 3. Finish off; weave in all ends.

Assembling
Alternating panels, place panels side by side with right side facing you and beg edge of each panel at same end of afghan. To join 2 panels, hold yarn at back of work and work sl sts on right side, alternating from edge to edge as follows. Use smaller size hook and join yarn with a sl st in st at bottom edge of right panel. Insert hook in corresponding st at bottom edge of left panel, hook yarn from beneath work and draw up through work and lp on hook [sl st made]. Sl st in next st on right panel, then sl st in corresponding st on left panel. Continue working in this manner (alternating sl sts from edge to edge) until panels are joined; finish off. Join rem panels in same manner.

Edging
With right side facing and working from **left to right,** use smaller size hook and work one row in reverse sc (see **Figs 10 and 11**) evenly spaced (approx every other row) across each long edge of afghan.

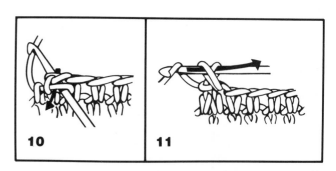

Fringe
Following *Fringe* instructions on pages 9 and 10, make triple knot fringe. Cut 24" strands of yarn; use 8 strands for each knot of fringe. Tie knots evenly spaced (approx every 3rd st) across each short end of afghan. Then work double and triple knots per instructions; trim ends evenly.

crocheted
HIGHLAND GLEN
designed by Carol Wilson Mansfield

This striking plaid afghan with its appealing color scheme, is quick to crochet — made with 2 strands of yarn and size K hook. The vertical stripes are added later — worked with slip stitches, using 4 strands of yarn.

SIZE: Approx 44″ x 58″ before fringing

MATERIALS
Worsted weight yarn: 34 oz ecru;
                      16 oz maroon;
                      8 oz red;
                      8 oz gray
Size K aluminum crochet hook (or size required for gauge)
Materials Note: Yarn is used doubled throughout patt, excluding vertical stripes.

GAUGE: With 2 strands of yarn in dc,
        9 sts = 4″; 8 rows = 5½″

INSTRUCTIONS

With 2 strands of ecru, ch 101 *loosely*.

Row 1 (right side): Dc in 4th ch from hook and in each of next 5 chs; ***(ch 1, sk one ch, dc in next ch) 3 times; dc in each of next 2 chs, ch 1, sk one ch, dc in each of next 11 chs; ch 1, sk one ch, dc in each of next 3 chs; (ch 1, sk one ch, dc in next ch) 3 times *** ; dc in each of next 26 chs; rep from * to * once, dc in each of last 6 chs.

Row 2 (patt row): Ch 3, turn; dc in each of next 6 dc; *** (ch 1, dc in next dc) 3 times; dc in each of next 2 dc; ch 1, dc in each of next 11 dc; ch 1, dc in each of next 3 dc; (ch 1, dc in next dc) 3 times *** ; dc in each of next 26 dc; rep from * to * once, dc in each of last 5 dc; dc in top of ch-3.

Rows 3 and 4: Rep Row 2, twice.

Continuing to use 2 strands of yarn, rep Row 2 in the following color sequence [**To Change Colors: Work last dc of row until 2 lps rem on hook, finish off old color; with new color, YO and draw through both lps on hook = color changed.**]:

> 1 row each maroon, ecru, maroon, ecru and maroon (5 rows total)
> 3 rows ecru
> 1 row each red, ecru, maroon, ecru and maroon (5 rows total)
> 3 rows ecru
> 1 row gray
> 7 rows ecru
> 1 row gray
> 3 rows ecru
> 1 row each maroon, ecru, maroon, ecru and red (5 rows total)
> 3 rows ecru
> 1 row each maroon, ecru, maroon, ecru and maroon (5 rows total)
> 3 rows ecru
> 1 row each red, ecru, maroon, ecru and maroon (5 rows total)
> 3 rows ecru
> 1 row gray
> 7 rows ecru
> 1 row gray
> 3 rows ecru
> 1 row each maroon, ecru, maroon, ecru and red (5 rows total)
> 3 rows ecru
> 1 row each maroon, ecru, maroon, ecru and maroon (5 rows total)
> 4 rows ecru

When last row of color sequence is completed, finish off. Weave in all ends.

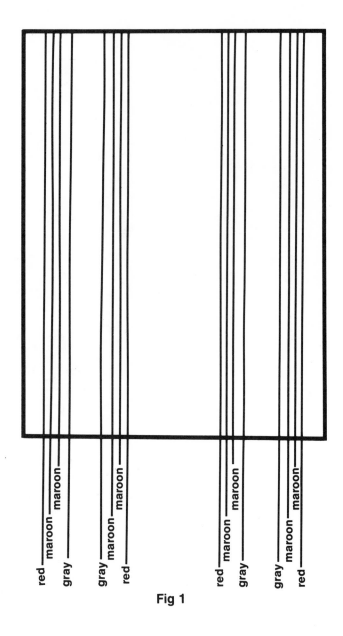

Fig 1

Vertical Stripes

Refer to color sequence in **Fig 1** and work each vertical stripe in ch-1 sps on right side of afghan as follows. With 4 strands of yarn, make slip knot on hook, leaving approx 8″ ends to be worked in later as part of fringe. Keeping yarn beneath work, beg at lower edge (along foundation chain) and work sl st in each ch-1 sp to top edge of afghan. [**To Work Sl St: Insert hook in ch-1 sp from front to back, hook 4 strands of yarn from beneath work and draw through work and lp on hook = sl st made.**] Be sure to work sl sts VERY LOOSELY so as not to pucker or distort afghan. Finish off, leaving approx 8″ ends to be worked in later as part of fringe.

Fringe

Following *Fringe* instructions on page 9, make single knot fringe. Cut 14″ strands of each color. Use 6 strands for each ecru knot and 4 strands for each red, gray and maroon knot. Tie matching knots evenly spaced (approx every other st) across each short end of afghan [add yarn ends to knot at end of each vertical stripe].

crocheted
EMPRESS COVERLET
designed by Mary Thomas

This beautiful design, made with heavy weight thread, is sure to be a family heirloom and treasure. It can also be made with bedspread weight thread, using size 5 steel crochet hook — adding more squares for desired size.

SIZES: Twin size measures approx 58″ x 98″
Full size measures approx 74″ x 98″

MATERIALS
American Thread Empress Quick Crochet Thread in White: 65 balls for twin size; or 84 balls for full size
Size D aluminum crochet hook (or size required for gauge)

GAUGE: One square = 8″

INSTRUCTIONS

Square
(Make 84 squares for twin size; or 108 squares for full size.)

Ch 6, join with a sl st to form a ring. [**Note:** All following rnds are worked on right side.]

Rnd 1: Work beg cluster in ring [**To Work Beg Cluster: Ch 3; YO, insert hook in ring and draw up ½″ lp; (YO and draw through 2 lps on hook) twice = beg cluster made.**]; * ch 2, work cluster in ring [**To Work Cluster: (YO, insert hook in ring and draw up ½″ lp; YO and draw through 2 lps on hook) twice; YO and draw through 3 lps on hook = cluster made.**]; rep from * 6 times more; ch 2, join with a sl st in top of beg cluster = 8 clusters.

Rnd 2: * Sc in next ch-2 sp, ch 4; work (sc, ch 9, sc) in next ch-2 sp, ch 4; rep from * 3 times more, join with a sl st in beg sc.

Rnd 3: Ch 1, * sc in next ch-4 sp, work (8 dc, ch 2, 8 dc) in ch-9 sp for petal; sc in next ch-4 sp, ch 5; rep from * 3 times more, join with a sl st in beg sc.

Rnd 4: Sl st in each of next 2 dc; ch 3, dc in each of next 6 dc; work (dc, ch 2, dc) in ch-2 sp at tip of petal; * dc in each of next 7 dc, sk last dc of petal; sc in 3rd ch of ch-5, sk first dc of next petal, dc in each of next 7 dc, work (dc, ch 2, dc) in ch-2 sp at tip of next petal; rep from * twice more; dc in each of next 7 dc, sk last dc of petal, sc in 3rd ch of ch-5; join with a sl st in top of beg ch-3.

Rnd 5: * Sc in next dc, (ch 4, sk 2 dc, sc in next dc) twice; work (sc, ch 3, sc) in ch-2 sp at tip of petal; sc in next dc, (ch 4, sk 2 dc, sc in next dc) twice; sk last dc of petal, sc in next sc, sk first dc of next petal; rep from * 3 times more, join with a sl st in beg sc.

Rnd 6: Sl st in next ch-4 sp, ch 3, 3 dc in same sp; 4 dc in next ch-4 sp, * work (2 dc, ch 3, 2 dc) in ch-3 sp at tip of petal for corner; (4 dc in next ch-4 sp) twice, sk next sc, dc in next sc; sk next sc, (4 dc in next ch-4 sp) twice; rep from * 3 times more, ending last rep by joining with a sl st in top of beg ch-3 instead of working (4 dc in next ch-4 sp) twice.

Rnd 7: Ch 3, dc in each of next 9 dc; * work (2 dc, ch 3, 2 dc) in corner sp, dc in each of next 21 dc; rep from * 3 times more, ending last rep by working dc in each of next 11 dc instead of 21 dc; join with a sl st in top of beg ch-3.

Rnd 8: Ch 4, (sk one dc, dc in next dc, ch 1) 5 times; * sk next dc, work (dc, ch 1, dc, ch 3, dc, ch 1, dc) in corner sp; ch 1, (sk one dc, dc in next dc, ch 1) 12 times; rep from * 3 times more, ending last rep by working)sk one dc, dc in next dc, ch 1) 6 times instead of 12 times; join with a sl st in 3rd ch of beg ch-4.

Rnd 9: Sl st in next ch-1 sp, work beg cluster (see Rnd 1) in same sp; (ch 1, cluster in next ch-1 sp) 6 times; ch 1, * work (cluster, ch 3, cluster) in corner sp, ch 1; (cluster in next ch-1 sp, ch 1) 15 times; rep from * 3 times more, ending last rep by working (cluster in next ch-1 sp, ch 1) 8 times instead of 15 times; join with a sl st in top of beg cluster.

Rnd 10: Sl st in next ch-1 sp, ch 4; (dc in next ch-1 sp, ch 1) 6 times; * work (dc, ch 1, dc, ch 3, dc, ch 1, dc) in corner sp, ch 1; (dc in next ch-1 sp, ch 1) 16 times; rep from * 3 times more, ending last rep by working (dc in next ch-1 sp, ch 1) 9 times instead of 16 times; join with a sl st in 3rd ch of beg ch-4.

Rnd 11: Ch 2, (hdc in next ch-1 sp, hdc in next dc) 8 times; * work (hdc, 2 dc, hdc) in corner sp; (hdc in next dc, hdc in ch-1 sp) 19 times, hdc in next dc; rep from * 3 times more, ending last rep by working (hdc in next dc, hdc in ch-1 sp) 11 times instead of 19 times; join with a sl st in top of beg ch-2. Finish off; weave in all ends.

Assembling

Twin size is 7 squares wide by 12 squares long; full size is 9 squares wide by 12 squares long.

Arrange squares with right side facing you and last st of each square facing same edge of coverlet. To join, hold two squares with right sides tog. Carefully matching sts and working in **outer lps only**, beg in dc at corner and sew with overcast st in corresponding sts **(Fig 1)** across, ending in dc at next corner. Join squares in rows; then sew rows tog, being sure each 4-corner junction is firmly joined. Weave in all ends. Lightly steam press joinings on wrong side.

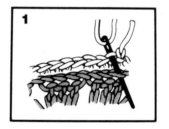

Edging

With right side facing, join with a sl st in any joining (between squares).

Rnd 1: Ch 4; counting each joining as one st, work (dc in next st, ch 1, sk one st) across each side edge; and in each st at each outer corner, work (dc in next st, ch 1); join with a sl st in 3rd ch of beg ch-4.

Rnd 2: Ch 2, work hdc in each ch-1 sp and in each dc around; join with a sl st in top of beg ch-2. Finish off; weave in all ends.

knitted ripple
AUTUMN GLORY

designed by Jean Leinhauser

SIZE: Approx 38″ x 62″

MATERIALS
Worsted weight yarn: 6 oz rust;
                           12 oz gold;
                           16 oz. rust/tan/gold ombre
**Size 10½, 36″ circular knitting needle (or size
    required for gauge)**

GAUGE: In stock st, 4 sts = 1″

PATTERN STITCH (multiple of 12 sts +3)

Row 1: K1; sl 1 as to knit, K1, PSSO; * K9, double dec [**To Work Double Dec: Insert right-hand needle into next 2 sts as if to knit (Fig 1); do not knit, but instead sl these 2 sts tog to right-hand needle (Fig 2); K1, pass both sl sts tog over knit st = double dec made.**]; rep from * to last 12 sts; K9, K2 tog, K1.

Row 2: P6; * double inc [**To Work Double Inc: Purl next st but leave st on left-hand needle; YO and purl again in same st (Fig 3); now sl st off left-hand needle = double inc made.**], P9; rep from * to last 7 sts; double inc, P6. [**Note:** *On next row, work each YO as one st.*]

Rep Rows 1 and 2 for patt.

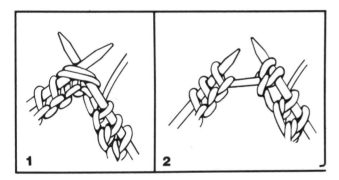

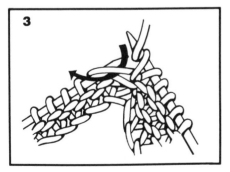

INSTRUCTIONS

With gold, CO 207 sts *loosely*. Do not join; work back and forth in rows. Work in Pattern Stitch using the following 26-row color sequence:

         4 rows gold
         2 rows rust
         2 rows gold
         2 rows rust
         4 rows gold
        12 rows ombre

Rep 26-row color sequence, 9 times more; then work 14 more rows as follows:
         4 rows gold
         2 rows rust
         2 rows gold
         2 rows rust
         4 rows gold

BO all sts *loosely*. Weave in all ends. On wrong side, lightly steam ends and side edges to keep from curling.

Fisherman knit
ARAN ISLES
designed by Wanda Parker

Inspired by the sweater patterns which were knitted by the village women off the west coast of Ireland — patterns relating rather poetically to the daily lives of the fisherfolk — this beautiful and classic design will delight the experienced knitter.

SIZE: Approx 50″ x 60″ before fringing

MATERIALS
Worsted weight yarn: 60 oz ecru
Size 9, 14″ straight knitting needles (or size required for gauge)
2 Cable needles
Size I aluminum crochet hook (for edging only)

GAUGE: In stock st, 9 sts = 2″; 6 rows = 1″

FISHERMAN PATTERN STITCHES

ROPE CABLE (worked on 6 sts or 11 sts)

Row 1 (cable twist row): P1; * sl next 2 sts onto cable needle and hold at FRONT of work; knit next 2 sts, then K2 from cable needle; P1. [**Note: For 11-st pattern, rep from * once more.**]

Row 2 (wrong side): K1; * P4, K1. [**Note: For 11-st pattern, rep from * once more.**]

Rep Rows 1 and 2 for patt.

ANTLER CABLE (worked on 10 sts)

Row 1 (cable twist row): P2; sl next 2 sts onto cable needle and hold at BACK of work; knit next st, then K2 from cable needle; sl next st to cable needle and hold at FRONT of work; knit next 2 sts, then K1 from cable needle; P2.

Row 2 (wrong side): K2, P6, K2.

Row 3: P2, K6, P2.

Row 4: Rep Row 2.

Rep Rows 1 through 4 for patt.

HOURGLASS CABLE (worked on 24 sts)

Row 1 (right side): P6, FC (front cross) [**To Work Front Cross: Sl next 2 sts onto cable needle and hold at FRONT of work; purl next 2 sts, then K2 from cable needle = FC made.**]; K4, BC (back cross) [**To Work Back Cross: Sl next 2 sts onto cable needle and hold at BACK of work; knit next 2 sts, then P2 from cable needle = BC made.**], P6.

Row 2: K8, P8, K8.

Row 3: P8, K8, P8.

Row 4: Rep Row 2.

Row 5: P8; sl next 2 sts onto cable needle and hold at FRONT of work; sl next 4 sts onto 2nd cable needle and hold at BACK of work; knit next 2 sts, then K4 from 2nd cable needle, then K2 from first cable needle; P8.

Row 6: Rep Row 2.

Row 7: P6, BC; K4, FC, P6.

Row 8: K6, P2; K2, P4, K2; P2, K6.

Row 9: P4, BC; P2, K4, P2; FC, P4.

Row 10: K4, P2; K4, P4, K4; P2, K4.

Row 11: (P2, BC) twice; (FC, P2) twice.

Row 12: K2, (P2, K4) 3 times; P2, K2.

Row 13: (BC, P2) twice; (P2, FC) twice.

Row 14: P2, K4; P2, K8, P2; K4, P2.

Row 15: K2, P4; K2, P8, K2; P4, K2.

Rows 16 through 19: Rep Rows 14 and 15, twice.

Row 20: Rep Row 14.

Row 21: (FC, P2) twice; (P2, BC) twice.

Row 22: Rep Row 12.

Row 23: (P2, FC) twice; (BC, P2) twice.

Row 24: Rep Row 10.

Row 25: P4, FC; P2, K4, P2; BC, P4.

Row 26: Rep Row 8.

Rep Rows 1 through 26 for patt.

HONEYCOMB (worked on 60 sts)

Row 1: * K2, BKC (back knit cross) [**To Work Back Knit Cross: Sl next 2 sts onto cable needle and hold at BACK of work; knit next 2 sts, then K2 from cable needle = BKC made.**]; FKC (front knit cross) [**To Work Front Knit Cross: Sl next 2 sts onto cable needle and hold at FRONT of work; knit next 2 sts, then K2 from cable needle = FKC made.**], K2; rep from * 4 times more.

Row 2 (wrong side): Purl.

Row 3: * BKC, K4, FKC; rep from * 4 times more.

Row 4: Purl.

Row 5: Knit.

Row 6: Purl.

Row 7: * FKC, K4, BKC; rep from * 4 times more.

Row 8: Purl.

Row 9: * K2, FKC; BKC, K2; rep from * across.

Rows 10, 11 and 12: Rep Rows 4, 5 and 6.

Rep Rows 1 through 12 for patt.

SCATTERED OATS (worked on 33 sts)

Row 1 (right side): K2; * (keeping yarn to back of work) sl 1 as to purl, K3; rep from * 7 times more, ending last rep by working K2 instead of K3.

Row 2: P2; * (keeping yarn to front of work) sl 1 as to purl, P3; rep from * 7 times more, ending last rep by working P2 instead of P3.

Row 3: * Sl next 2 sts onto cable needle and hold at BACK of work; knit next st (sl st), then K2 from cable needle, K1; rep from * 7 times more, ending last rep by working K2 instead of K1.

Row 4: Purl.

Row 5: Rep Row 1.

Row 6: Rep Row 2.

Row 7: K1; * K1, sl next st (sl st) onto cable needle and hold at FRONT of work; knit next 2 sts, then K1 from cable needle; rep from * 7 times more.

Row 8: Purl.

Rep Rows 1 through 8 for patt.

AFGHAN INSTRUCTIONS

Panel A (between center and side-edge panels) (Make 2)

CO 58 sts. Purl one row; then establish patterns as follows.

Row 1 (right side): [**Note:** *Work Row 1 of each Patt St.*] K1; **Rope Cable:** 6 sts; **Antler Cable:** 10 sts; **Hourglass Cable:** 24 sts; **Antler Cable:** 10 sts; **Rope Cable:** 6 sts; K1.

Keeping one st at each edge in garter st (knit edge st on each row), work even in patterns as established until 14 repeats of Hourglass Cable have been completed, ending by working Row 5 of Hourglass Cable, and Row 1 each of Antler Cable and Rope Cable. BO all sts in purl; weave in all ends.

Panel B (center panel)
(Make 1)

CO 74 sts. Purl one row; then establish patterns as follows.

Row 1 (right side): [**Note:** *Work Row 1 of each Patt St.*] K1; **Rope Cable:** 6 sts; **Honeycomb:** 60 sts; **Rope Cable:** 6 sts; K1.

Keeping one st at each edge in garter st, work even in patterns as established until panel measures same as Panel A, ending by working Row 9 of Honeycomb Patt, and Row 1 of Rope Cable. BO all sts in purl; weave in all ends.

Panel C (side-edge panel)
(Make 2)

CO 57 sts. Purl one row; then establish patterns as follows.

Row 1 (right side): [**Note:** *Work Row 1 of each Patt St.*] K1; **Rope Cable:** 11 sts; **Scattered Oats:** 33 sts; **Rope Cable:** 11 sts; K1.

Keeping one st at each edge in garter st, work even in patterns as established until panel measures same as Panel A, ending by working Row 1 each of Scattered Oats Patt and Rope Cable. BO all sts in purl; weave in all ends.

Assembling

Position panels side by side, having Honeycomb panel (Panel B) at center and Scattered Oats panel (Panel C) at each end. Be sure to have CO edge of each panel at same end of afghan. Carefully matching garter st edges, sew (whipstitch) panels tog.

Edging

With right side facing, work one rnd in sc evenly spaced around afghan (work 3 sc in each outer corner). Then work one row in dc (work one st in each sc) across each short end of afghan. Weave in all ends.

Fringe

Following *Fringe* instructions on pages 9 and 10, make triple knot fringe. Cut 16″ strands of yarn; use 6 strands for each knot of fringe. Tie knots evenly spaced across each short end of afghan; then work double and triple knots per instructions. Trim ends evenly.

crocheted
CHRISTMAS GRANNY
designed by Jean Leinhauser

SIZE: Approx 44" x 66" before fringing

MATERIALS
Worsted weight yarn: 10 oz red;
                     24 oz light green;
                     24 oz dark green

Size G aluminum crochet hook (or size required for gauge)

GAUGE: One square = 5½"

INSTRUCTIONS

Square (make 96)
With red, ch 5, join with a sl st to form a ring.

Rnd 1 (right side): Ch 3, 2 dc in ring; (ch 2, 3 dc in ring) 3 times, ch 2; join with a sl st in top of beg ch-3.

Rnd 2: Do not turn; sl st in each of next 2 dc and into ch-2 sp; ch 3, (2 dc, ch 2, 3 dc) in same sp; * work (3 dc, ch 2, 3 dc) all in next ch-2 sp; rep from * twice more, join with a sl st in top of beg ch-3. Finish off.

Rnd 3: With right side facing, join lt green with a sl st in any ch-2 sp; ch 3, (2 dc, ch 2, 3 dc) in same sp for first corner; * 3 dc between next two 3-dc groups for side, work (3 dc, ch 2, 3 dc) in next ch-2 sp for corner; rep from * twice more; 3 dc between next two 3-dc groups for last side, join with a sl st in top of beg ch-3. Finish off.

Rnd 4: With right side facing, join dk green with a sl st in any ch-2 corner sp; ch 3, (2 dc, ch 2, 3 dc) in same sp; * 3 dc between each pair of 3-dc groups along side, work (3 dc, ch 2, 3 dc) in next corner sp; rep from * twice more; 3 dc between each pair of 3-dc groups along last side, join with a sl st in top of beg ch-3. Do not finish off.

Rnd 5: Do not turn; sl st in each of next 2 dc and into corner sp; ch 3, (2 dc, ch 2, 3 dc) in same sp; * 3 dc between each pair of 3-dc groups along side, work (3 dc, ch 2, 3 dc) in next corner sp; rep from * twice more; 3 dc between each pair of 3-dc groups along last side, join with a sl st in top of beg ch-3. Finish off.

Rnd 6: With lt green, rep Rnd 4. Finish off; weave in all ends.

Assembling
Afghan is 8 squares wide by 12 squares long. To join, hold two squares with right sides tog. Thread matching yarn into tapestry needle. Carefully matching sts across, beg in ch st at corner and sew with overcast st in **outer lps only (Fig 1)** across side, ending in ch st at next corner. Join squares in rows; then sew rows tog, being careful to join each 4-corner junction securely. Lightly steam press joinings on wrong side, if desired.

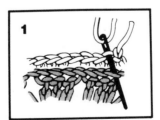

Fringe
Following *Fringe* instructions on page 9, make single knot fringe. Cut 12" strands each of lt and dk green. Use 3 strands each of lt green and dk green for each knot of fringe. Tie one knot in each sp (between each pair of 3-dc groups and in each corner sp) along each short end of afghan.

crochet filet
SPRING FLOWER

Adapted from a design in an antique needlework book, this magnificent design (featured on our jacket cover) revives the lovely old art of filet crochet. If you've been afraid to try filet, our new method of instructions makes it a breeze. This is not a difficult project, but does require a good bit of time to complete — time worth investing in a piece sure to become a family heirloom.

SIZE: Approx 48″ x 72″ before fringing

MATERIALS
Worsted weight yarn: 52 oz ecru
Size G aluminum crochet hook (or size required for gauge)

GAUGE: In dc, 15 sts = 4″; 15 rows = 8″

FILET CHART INSTRUCTIONS

Filet design is worked from a chart of squares. On each odd-numbered row (right side of work), work chart from right to left; on each even-numbered row (wrong side of work), work chart from left to right.

Work each row of chart (beg with Row 2) as follows:
Each vertical line as one dc (Fig 1). Work ch 3 for first vertical line; then work each following dc (vertical line) in dc (vertical line) in row below, ending by working dc in top of ch-3 for last vertical line.

Fig 1

Each open (non-shaded) sp [between two vertical lines] as one ch (Fig 2). In row below, you will skip either a ch-1 sp (open sp) or one dc (filled-in sp).

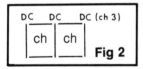

Fig 2

Each filled-in (shaded) sp [between two vertical lines] as one dc (Fig 3). Work dc either in ch-1 (ch-1 — open sp) or in dc (filled-in sp) of row below.

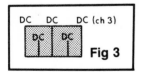

Fig 3

AFGHAN INSTRUCTIONS

Ch 183 *loosely*.

Row 1 (right side): Dc in 4th ch from hook and in each rem ch across = 181 dc. [**Note:** *Ch-3 counts as one dc throughout patt.*]

Row 2: Ch 3, turn; dc in each of next 2 dc; * ch 1, sk one dc, dc in next dc; rep from * to last 2 sts, dc in next dc, dc in top of ch-3.

Row 3: Ch 3, turn; dc in each of next 2 dc, (ch 1, sk ch-1 sp, dc in next dc) 10 times; (dc in ch-1 sp, dc in next dc) 4 times; ch 1, sk ch-1 sp, dc in next dc; (dc in ch-1 sp, dc in next dc) twice; (ch 1, sk ch-1 sp, dc in next dc) 3 times; (dc in ch-1 sp, dc in next dc) 3 times; (ch 1, sk ch-1 sp, dc in next dc) 4 times; dc in ch-1 sp, dc in next dc; (ch 1, sk ch-1 sp, dc in next dc) 13 times; (dc in ch-1 sp, dc in next dc) 6 times; (ch 1, sk ch-1 sp, dc in next dc) 13 times; dc in ch-1 sp, dc in next dc; (ch 1, sk ch-1 sp, dc in next dc) 4 times; (dc in ch-1 sp, dc in next dc) 3 times; (ch 1, sk ch-1 sp, dc in next dc) 3 times; (dc in ch-1 sp, dc in next dc) twice; ch 1, sk ch-1 sp, dc in next dc; (dc in ch-1 sp, dc in next dc) 4 times; (ch 1, sk ch-1 sp, dc in next dc) 10 times; dc in next dc, dc in top of ch-3.

Now refer to chart in **Fig 4.** You have just completed the first 3 rows; compare your work with the chart. Now continue working only from the chart (see preceding Filet Chart Instructions). Beg with Row 4 and work through Row 135. At end of last row, finish off; weave in all ends.

Fringe
Following *Fringe* instructions on page 9, make single knot fringe. Cut 16″ strands of yarn; use 4 strands for each knot of fringe. Tie knots evenly spaced (approx every other st) across each short end of afghan.

Fig 4

Row 135

Chapter 4

Crochet Potpourri

crocheted
SNOWFLOWERS
designed by Barbara Retzke

Squares, made with an interesting petal stitch combined with a cluster stitch, are joined to make this beautiful afghan.

SIZE: Approx 55″ x 70″ before fringing

MATERIALS
Sport weight yarn: 44 oz white;
                              2 oz light blue;
                              4 oz light green
Size F aluminum crochet hook (or size required for gauge)

GAUGE: One square = 7¾″

INSTRUCTIONS
Square (make 63)
[**Note:** *All rnds are worked on right side.*]

With blue, ch 5, join with a sl st to form a ring

Rnd 1: Pull up lp on hook to ½″; * work CL (cluster) in ring [**To Work Cluster: YO, insert hook in ring or sp and**

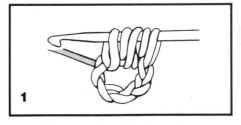

pull ½″ lp; **YO, insert hook in same ring or sp and pull up another ½″ lp [5 lps now on hook — Fig 1]; YO and draw through first 4 lps only; then YO and draw through rem 2 lps on hook = CL made.**], ch 2; rep from * 7 times more; join with a sl st in top of beg CL **(Fig 2)**. Finish off.

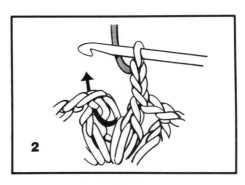

Rnd 2: With right side facing, join green with a sl st in any sp (between CL); pull up lp on hook to ½"; beg in same sp, work (CL, ch 2) twice in each sp around; join with a sl st in top of beg CL = 16 CL. Finish off.

Rnd 3: With right side facing, join white with a sl st in any sp; pull up lp on hook to ½"; work (CL, ch 2, CL, ch 1) in same sp for first corner; * beg in same sp, work (PS — petal stitch) 4 times for side [**To Work PS: YO, draw up ½" lp in same sp (where last st was completed); draw up ½" lp in next sp (between sts); YO and draw through all 4 lps on hook (Fig 3), ch 1 = PS made.**];

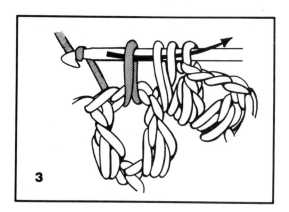

work (CL, ch 2, CL, ch 1) in same sp (where last st was worked); rep from * twice more; beg in same sp, work (PS) 4 times for last side, ending last st in beg corner sp; join with a sl st in top of beg CL. Do not finish off.

Rnd 4: Sl st into beg ch-2 corner sp and pull up lp on hook to ½"; work (CL, ch 2, CL, ch 1) in same sp; * beg in same sp and work 6 PS across side, ending in next ch-2 corner sp; work (CL, ch 2, CL, ch 1) in same sp; rep from * twice more; beg in same sp and work 6 PS across last side, ending last st in beg ch-2 corner sp; join with a sl st in top of beg CL. Do not finish off.

Rnds 5 through 9: Work in same manner as Rnd 4, having 2 more PS across each side. At end of Rnd 9, you should have 16 PS across each side. Finish off, leaving approx 16" sewing length. Weave in ends.

Assembling
Afghan is 7 squares wide by 9 squares long. To join, hold 2 squares with right sides tog. Thread yarn into tapestry needle. Carefully matching corresponding sts across and working in **outer lps only (Fig 4),** sew with overcast st across side. Join squares in rows; then sew rows tog, being sure that all four-corner junctions are firmly joined.

Fringe
Following *Fringe* instructions on page 9, make single knot fringe. Cut 14" strands of white; use 3 strands for each knot of fringe. Tie knots evenly spaced (in each sp and in each joining) across each short end of afghan.

crocheted
GOLDEN AMBER

designed Joan Kokaska

SIZE: Approx 45″ x 63″

MATERIALS
Worsted weight yarn: 8 oz white;
8 oz green;
22 oz amber;
16 oz rust

Size G aluminum crochet hook (or size required for gauge)

GAUGE: One square = 4½″

INSTRUCTIONS

Square A (make 84)
[**Note:** All rnds are worked on right side.]

With green, ch 5, join with a sl st to form a ring.

Rnd 1: Ch 3, 2 dc in ring; (ch 3, 3 dc in ring) 3 times, ch 3; join with a sl st in top of beg ch-3. Finish off. [**Note:** *Ch-3 counts as one dc throughout patt.*]

Rnd 2: With right side facing, join white with a sl st in any ch-3 sp; ch 3, (dc, ch 3, 2 dc) in same sp as joining [beg corner made]; dc in next dc, tr in base of next dc [**To**

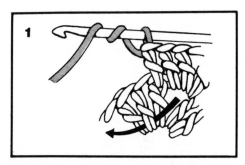

1

Work Tr: YO twice, insert hook under 2 threads at base of next dc (Fig 1); hook yarn and draw lp through st (4 lps now on hook); (YO and draw through 2 lps on hook) 3 times = tr made.]; dc in next dc [first side completed]; * (2 dc, ch 3, 2 dc) in next ch-3 sp [next corner made]; dc in next dc, tr in base of next dc, dc in next dc [next side made]; rep from * twice more, join with a sl st in top of beg ch-3. Finish off.

Rnd 3: With right side facing, join rust with a sl st in any ch-3 corner sp; ch 3, (2 dc, ch 3, 3 dc) in same sp; sk 2 dc, 3 dc in sp between sts (skipped dc and next dc — **Fig 2);**

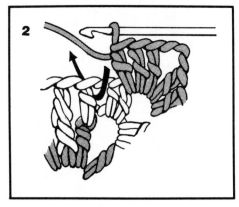

2

sk next 3 sts (dc, tr, dc), 3 dc in sp between sts (skipped dc and next dc); * (3 dc, ch 3, 3 dc) in next ch-3 corner sp; sk 2 dc, 3 dc in sp between sts (skipped dc and next dc); sk next 3 sts (dc, tr, dc), 3 dc in sp between sts (skipped dc and next dc); rep from * twice more, join with a sl st in top of beg ch-3. Finish off.

Rnd 4: With right side facing, join amber with a sl st in any ch-3 corner sp; ch 3, (dc, ch 3, 2 dc) in same sp; (dc in next dc, tr in base of next dc, dc in next dc) 4 times; * (2 dc, ch 3, 2 dc) in next ch-3 corner sp; (dc in next dc, tr in base of next dc, dc in next dc) 4 times; rep from * twice more, join with a sl st in top of beg ch-3. Finish off; weave in all ends.

Square B (make 56)
Following instructions for Square A, beg with white and work rnds in the following color sequence:
   Rnd 1: White
   Rnd 2: Green
   Rnd 3: Rust
   Rnd 4: Amber

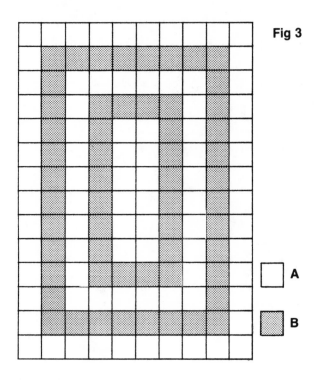

Fig 3

A

B

Assembling
Position squares as shown in **Fig 3,** having right side of each square facing up. To join, hold two squares with right sides facing. Thread amber into tapestry needle. Carefully matching corresponding sts across side, beg in center ch of corner and sew with overcast st in **outer lps only (Fig 4)** across, ending in center ch of next corner. Join squares into rows; then sew rows tog, being sure that all four-corner junctions are firmly joined.

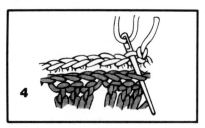

4

crocheted
HARVEST FESTIVAL

designed by Verna Williams

Long strips, made with shell stitches in ombre yarn and edged in brown and orange, join to form this striking design, with scalloped edges at top and bottom.

SIZE: Approx 56″ x 69″

MATERIALS
Worsted weight yarn: 12 oz light orange;
                        16 oz brown;
                        16 oz ombre in shades of orange, olive green and brown
Sizes G and H aluminum crochet hooks (or sizes required for gauge)
Size F aluminum crochet hook (for joining only)

GAUGE: With size H hook,
           one shell (3 dc, ch 3, 3 dc) = 1½″
           With size G hook in sc, 4 sts = 1″

INSTRUCTIONS
Strip (make 13)
With size H hook (or size required for gauge) and ombre, ch 6, join with a sl st to form a ring.

Row 1: Ch 3, (2 dc, ch 2, 3 dc) in ring [beg shell made].

Row 2: Ch 3, turn; work a shell (3 dc, ch 2, 3 dc) in ch-2 sp of shell in prev row; dc in top of ch-3 at end of row.

Rep Row 2 until strip measures approx 66″ long, or 3″ less than desired length. Finish off; then continue with edging around strip as follows.

Edging
Hold strip with side edge across top and last shell worked to your right. With size G hook (or size required for gauge), join brown with a sl st in any sp between shells (sp under dc or ch-3 at end of row).

Rnd 1 (right side): Ch 3, 2 dc in same sp; work 3 dc in each sp between shells across side; work 15 dtr (double

triple crochet) in ring (where beg shell was worked) [**To Work Dtr: YO 3 times; insert hook in sp and draw up a lp (5 lps now on hook); (YO and draw through 2 lps on hook) 4 times = dtr made.**]; work 3 dc in each sp between shells across side; work 15 dtr in ch-2 sp of shell at end of strip (last shell made); work 3 dc in each rem sp between shells across side; join with a sl st in top of beg ch-3.

Rnd 2: Do not turn; with last rnd facing you and size G hook, join orange with a sl st in any dc; ch 1, sc in same dc and in each dc to 15-dtr group at end; sc in each of next 3 dtr, (2 sc in next dtr, sc in each of next 2 dtr) 4 times; sc in each dc across to 15-dtr group at other end; sc in each of next 3 dtr, (2 sc in next dtr, sc in each of next 2 dtr) 4 times; sc in each rem dc, join with a sl st in beg sc. Finish off.

Assembling
To join, hold two strips with wrong sides tog, end with 15-dtr group (worked into last shell of strip) to your left, and side edge across top. Carefully matching sts and working in **back lp only** of corresponding sts across, join orange with a sl st in sc above first st of 15-dtr group at upper left-hand corner, ch 1. Working from **left to right** in reverse sc **(see Figs 1 and 2),** work one st in same st as joining and in each rem sc across side, ending in sc above last st of 15-dtr group at upper right-hand corner. Finish off. Join rem strips in same manner.

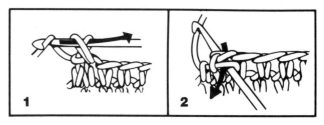

Edging
With right side facing and size G hook (or size required for gauge), join orange with a sl st in any sc at either side edge of afghan. Working from **left to right** in reverse sc, work one st in each st around afghan; join with a sl st in beg st. Finish off; weave in ends.

crocheted
DAISY FIELD
designed by Eleanor Denner

SIZE: Approx 44" x 60"

MATERIALS
Worsted weight yarn: 36 oz spring green;
                    12 oz white;
                    4 oz bright yellow
Size F aluminum crochet hook (or size required for gauge)

GAUGE: One Daisy Hexagon = 7¼" (measured across from side to side)

INSTRUCTIONS

Daisy Hexagon (make 50)
With yellow, ch 4, join with a sl st to form a ring.

Rnd 1 (wrong side): Ch 3, work 13 dc in ring; join with a sl st in top of beg ch-3. Finish off. [**Note:** *Ch-3 counts as one dc throughout patt.*]

Rnd 2: Turn; join white with a sl st in any dc; ch 3, dc in same st as joining, dc in next dc; * 2 dc in next dc, dc in next dc; rep from * 5 times more, join with a sl st in top of beg ch-3 = 21 dc (counting ch-3). Do not finish off.

Rnd 3: Ch 3, turn; dc in same st as joining, 3 dc in next dc, 2 dc in next dc; * 2 dc in next dc, 3 dc in next dc, 2 dc in next dc; rep from * 5 times more, join with a sl st in top of beg ch-3 = 49 dc.

Rnd 4: Ch 1, turn; * sc in next dc, sk 2 dc; work (4 dc, ch 2, 4 dc) in next dc (center dc of 3-dc group) for tip of petal; sk 2 dc, sc in next dc; rep from * 6 times more, ending last rep by working sc in top of ch-3 (where prev rnd was joined). Finish off.

Rnd 5: Do not turn; with right side of last rnd facing you, join green with a sl st in sp between any 2 sc; ch 1, sc in same sp as joining, ch 5; * working behind petal, sc in sp between next 2 sc, ch 5; rep from * 5 times more, join with a sl st in beg sc = 7 ch-5 sps. Do not finish off.

Rnd 6: Ch 5, turn; dc in same st as joining of prev rnd, 6 dc in next ch-5 sp; * (dc, ch 2, dc) in next sc, 6 dc in next ch-5 sp; rep from * 5 times more, join with a sl st in 3rd ch of beg ch-5 = 8 dc across each side (between ch-2 sps).

Rnd 7: Ch 3, turn; work dc in each dc around; and in each ch-2 sp, work (dc, ch 2, dc); join with a sl st in top of beg ch-3 = 10 dc across each side (between ch-2 sps).

Rnds 8 through 10: Rep Rnd 7, three times. At end of each rnd, you should have 2 more dc across each side (between ch-2 sps). At end of Rnd 10, you should have 16 dc across each side. Finish off; weave in all ends.

Half Hexagon (make 8)
With green, ch 4, join with a sl st to form a ring.

Row 1 (wrong side): Ch 3, dc in ring; (ch 2, 2 dc in ring) twice.

Row 2: Ch 3, turn; dc in each of **first** 2 dc, work (dc, ch 2, dc) in ch-2 sp; dc in each of next 2 dc, work (dc, ch 2, dc) in next ch-2 sp; dc in next dc, 2 dc in top of ch-3 = 4 dc across each side (between ch-2 sps). [**Note:** *Ch-3 counts as one dc.*]

Row 3: Ch 3, turn; dc in first dc and in each dc to ch-2 sp; work (dc, ch 2, dc) in ch-2 sp, dc in each dc to next ch-2 sp; work (dc, ch 2, dc) in ch-2 sp, dc in each dc to last dc (ch-3); 2 dc in top of ch-3 = 6 dc across each side (between ch-2 sps).

Rows 4 through 8: Rep Row 3, 5 times. At end of each row, you should have 2 more dc across each side. At end of Row 8, you should have 16 dc across each side. Finish off; weave in all ends.

Fig 1

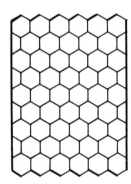

Assembling
Position motifs (daisy hexagons and half hexagons) as shown in **Fig 1**. To join, hold 2 motifs with right sides tog. Thread green into tapestry needle. Carefully matching corresponding sts across side, beg in ch st at right-hand edge and sew with overcast st in **outer lps only (Fig 2)** across, ending in ch st at left-hand edge. Continue to join sides of motifs tog in this manner. Weave in all ends.

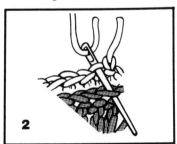

Edging
With green and right side facing, work one row in sc evenly spaced (approx one sc in each st and 2 sc in each row) across each side edge of afghan.

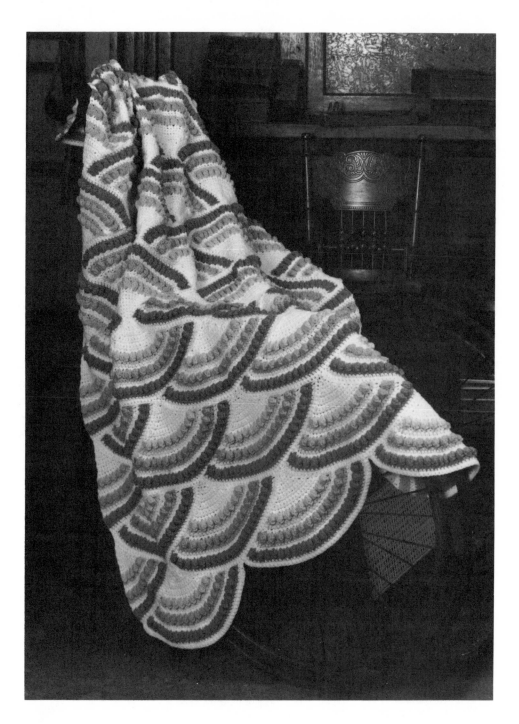

crocheted
CLAMSHELL

Shell motifs, which fan out from the center toward each end of the afghan, create this stunning design. Half motifs are added along side edges, filling in spaces between motifs.

SIZE: Approx 42″ x 58″

MATERIALS
American Thread Dawn Sayelle* Worsted Size Yarn:
       28 oz White;
       12 oz Baby Blue;
       14 oz Bluebell;
       16 oz True Blue
Size H aluminum crochet hook (or size required for gauge)

GAUGE: One Full Shell Motif measures as follows:

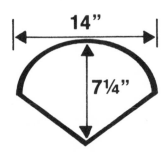

14"

7¼"

52

INSTRUCTIONS

Full Shell Motif (make 38)

With White, ch 2.

Row 1 (right side): Sc in 2nd ch from hook.

Row 2: Ch 1, turn; 3 sc in sc.

Row 3: Ch 1, turn; 2 sc in first sc, sc in next sc, 2 sc in last sc = 5 sc.

Row 4: Ch 1, turn; 2 sc in first sc, sc in each sc to last sc, 2 sc in last sc = 7 sc.

Rows 5 through 10: Rep Row 4, six times. At end of Row 10, you should have 19 sc. Finish off White.

Row 11: Turn; join Baby Blue with a sl st in first sc, ch 4; work PC (popcorn) in next sc [**To Work PC: Work 4 dc in st; drop lp from hook, insert hook in first dc of 4-dc group just made; then hook dropped lp and pull through lp on hook (Fig 1), ch 1 = PC made.**] ; * dc in next sc, PC in next sc; rep from * to last sc; dc in last sc = 9 PC.

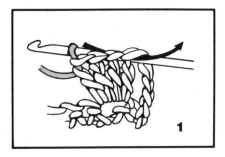

Row 12: Ch 1, turn; 2 sc in first dc; * sc in next PC, sc in next dc; 2 sc in next PC, sc in next dc; rep from * to last PC; sc in PC, 2 sc in 3rd ch of ch-4 = 25 sc. Finish off Baby Blue.

Row 13: Turn; join White with a sl st in first sc, ch 1; sc in each of first 2 sc, 2 sc in next sc; sc in each sc to last 3 sc; 2 sc in next sc, sc in each of last 2 sc = 27 sc.

Row 14: Ch 1, turn; sc in each of first 2 sc, 2 sc in next sc; sc in each sc to last 3 sc; 2 sc in next sc, sc in each of last 2 sc = 29 sc. Finish off White.

Row 15: With Bluebell, rep Row 11 = 14 PC.

Row 16: Ch 1, turn; sc in first dc, * sc in next PC, 2 sc in next dc; rep from * to last PC; 2 sc in last PC, sc in 3rd ch of ch-4 = 43 sc. Finish off Bluebell.

Rows 17 and 18: Rep Rows 13 and 14. At end of Row 18, you should have 47 sc. Finish off White.

Row 19: With True Blue, rep Row 11 = 23 PC.

Row 20: Ch 1, turn; sc in first dc and in next PC, 2 sc in next dc; sc in each rem PC and dc to last 3 sts; 2 sc in next dc, sc in last PC, sc in 3rd ch of ch-4 = 49 sc. Finish off True Blue.

Rows 21 and 22: Rep Rows 13 and 14. At end of Row 22, you should have 53 sc. Finish off White. Weave in all ends.

Left Half Motif (make 7)

With White, ch 2.

Row 1 (right side): Sc in 2nd ch from hook.

Row 2: Ch 1, turn; 2 sc in sc.

Row 3: Ch 1, turn; sc in first sc, 2 sc in next sc = 3 sc.

Row 4: Ch 1, turn; 2 sc in first sc, sc in each of next 2 sc = 4 sc.

Row 5: Ch 1, turn; sc in each of first 3 sc, 2 sc in last sc = 5 sc.

Row 6: Ch 1, turn; 2 sc in first sc, sc in each rem sc across = 6 sc.

Row 7: Ch 1, turn; sc in each sc to last sc, 2 sc in last sc = 7 sc.

Rows 8 and 9: Rep Rows 6 and 7. At end of Row 9, you should have 9 sc.

Row 10: Ch 1, turn; 2 sc in first sc, sc in each sc to last sc, 2 sc in last sc = 11 sc. Finish off White.

Row 11: Turn; join Baby Blue with a sl st in first sc, ch 4; PC in next sc, * dc in next sc, PC in next sc; rep from * to last sc; dc in last sc = 5 PC.

Row 12: Ch 1, turn; 2 sc in first dc; * sc in next PC, sc in dc; 2 sc in next PC, sc in next dc; rep from * to last PC; sc in PC, 2 sc in 3rd ch of ch-4 = 15 sc. Finish off Baby Blue.

Row 13: Turn; join White with a sl st in first sc, ch 1, sc in each sc to last sc; 2 sc in last sc = 16 sc.

Row 14: Ch 1, turn; 2 sc in first sc, sc in each rem sc across = 17 sc. Finish off White.

Row 15: With Bluebell, rep Row 11 = 8 PC.

Row 16: Ch 1, turn; sc in first dc; (sc in next PC, 2 sc in next dc) 5 times; (sc in next PC, sc in next dc) twice; sc in last PC, 2 sc in 3rd ch of ch-4 = 23 sc. Finish off Bluebell.

Rows 17 and 18: Rep Rows 13 and 14. At end of Row 14, you should have 25 sc. Finish off White.

Row 19: With True Blue, rep Row 11 = 12 PC.

Row 20: Ch 1, turn; 2 sc in first dc, sc in each PC and in each dc across, ending sc in 3rd ch of ch-4 = 26 sc. Finish off True Blue.

Rows 21 and 22: Rep Rows 13 and 14. At end of Row 22, you should have 28 sc. Finish off White. Weave in all ends.

Right Half Motif (make 7)

With White, ch 2.

Rows 1 and 2: Rep Rows 1 and 2 of Left Half Motif.

Row 3: Ch 1, turn; 2 sc in first sc, sc in last sc = 3 sc.

Row 4: Ch 1, turn; sc in each of first 2 sc, 2 sc in last sc = 4 sc.

Row 5: Ch 1, turn; 2 sc in first sc, sc in each of rem 3 sc = 5 sc.

Row 6: Ch 1, turn; sc in each sc to last sc, 2 sc in last sc = 6 sc.

Row 7: Ch 1, turn; 2 sc in first sc, sc in each rem sc across = 7 sc.

Rows 8 and 9: Rep prev Rows 6 and 7. At end of Row 9, you should have 9 sc.

Rows 10 through 12: Rep Rows 10 through 12 of Left Half Motif.

Row 13: Turn; join White with a sl st in first sc, ch 1; 2 sc in first sc, sc in each rem sc across = 16 sc.

Row 14: Ch 1, turn; sc in each sc across to last sc, 2 sc in last sc = 17 sc. Finish off White.

Rows 15 and 16: Rep Rows 15 and 16 of Left Half Motif.

Rows 17 and 18: Rep Rows 13 and 14 of **Right Half Motif.** At end of Row 18, you should have 25 sc. Finish off White.

Row 19: With True Blue, rep Row 11 of Left Half Motif = 12 PC.

Row 20: Ch 1, turn; sc in each dc and in each PC across, ending 2 sc in 3rd ch of ch-4 = 26 sc. Finish off True Blue.

Rows 21 and 22: Rep Rows 13 and 14 of **Right Half Motif.** At end of Row 22, you should have 28 sc. Finish off White. Weave in all ends.

Assembling

Arrange motifs as shown in **Fig 2.** With White, sew motifs tog. Steam press joinings on wrong side.

Fig 2

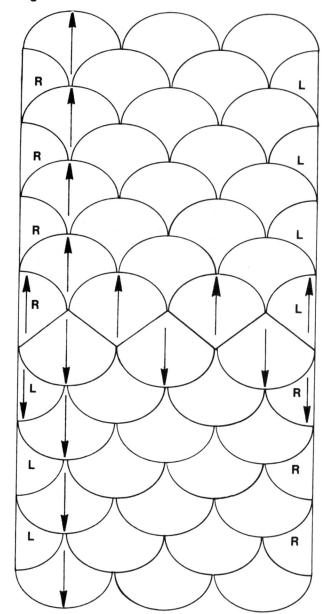

crocheted
FIESTA
designed by Jean Leinhauser

SIZE: Approx 45″ x 64″

MATERIALS
American Thread Dawn Sayelle* Knitting Worsted
  Size Yarn in 4-oz skeins:
        8 skeins Fisherman;
        2 skeins Orange;
        2 skeins Brt. Watermelon;
        2 skeins Turquoise
Size I aluminum crochet hook (or size required for
  gauge)

GAUGE: In hdc, 3 sts = 1″; 4 rows = 1½″

INSTRUCTIONS
With Orange, ch 145 *loosely.*
Row 1: Hdc in 2nd ch from hook and in each rem ch across = 144 hdc. [**Note:** *On following rows, do not count ch-2 as one hdc.*]
Row 2: Ch 2, turn; hdc in each hdc across.
Rows 3 and 4: Rep Row 2, twice. At end of Row 4, cut Orange, leaving 4″ end.
Row 5: With Brt. Watermelon, ch 1, turn; sc in each hdc across.
Row 6 (right side): Ch 3 (counts as first st), turn;* PC (popcorn) in next sc [**To Make PC: Work 5 dc in st; drop lp from hook, insert hook in first dc of 5-dc group just made; hook dropped lp and pull through lp on hook (Fig 1) = PC made.**]; ch 1, sk next sc; rep from * to last sc, dc in last sc = 71 PC.

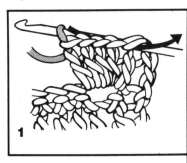

Row 7: Ch 1, turn; sc in first dc, * sc in ch-1, sc in top of PC; rep from * across, ending sc in top of ch-3 = 144 sc. Cut Brt. Watermelon, leaving 4″ end.
Row 8: With Fisherman, ch 2, turn; hdc in each sc across.
Rows 9 through 16: Rep Row 2, eight times. At end of Row 16, cut Fisherman.
Rows 17, 18 and 19: Rep Rows 5, 6 and 7. At end of Row 19, cut Brt. Watermelon.
Row 20: With Orange, ch 2, turn; hdc in each sc across.
Rows 21 through 23: Rep Row 2, three times. At end of Row 23, finish off Orange.
Row 24 (wrong side): With right side of last row just worked facing you, join Turquoise with a sc in st at upper right-hand corner; sc in each rem st across = 144 sc.

Row 25: Ch 3 (counts as first st), turn; * sk next sc, dc in next sc, dc in skipped sc **(Fig 2)**; rep from * to last sc, dc in last sc.
Row 26: Ch 1, turn; sc in each dc across, ending sc in top of ch-3 = 144 sc.
Row 27: Rep Row 25. Cut Turquoise.
Row 28: With Brt. Watermelon, rep Row 26.
Rows 29 and 30: Rep Rows 25 and 26.
Row 31: Rep Row 25. Cut Brt. Watermelon.
Row 32: With Turquoise, rep Row 26.
Rows 33 and 34: Rep Rows 25 and 26.
Row 35: Rep Row 25. Cut Turquoise.
Row 36: With Fisherman, rep Row 26.

Striped border is now completed. Continuing with Fisherman only, rep Rows 25 and 26 until work measures approx 48″ long, ending by working Row 25. Cut Fisherman; then work other striped border as follows. To avoid confusion, row numbers for this border will start again at Row 37.

Rows 37 through 40: With Turquoise, rep Rows 32 through 35. At end of Row 40; cut Turquoise.
Rows 41 through 44: With Brt. Watermelon, rep Rows 28 through 31. At end of Row 44, cut Brt. Watermelon.
Rows 45 through 48: With Turquoise, rep Rows 32 through 35. At end of Row 48, cut Turquoise.
Row 49: With Orange, ch 2, turn; hdc in each dc across, ending hdc in top of ch-3.
Rows 50 through 52: Rep Row 2, three times. At end of Row 52, cut Orange.
Rows 53, 54 and 55: With Brt. Watermelon, rep Rows 5, 6 and 7. At end of Row 55, cut Brt. Watermelon.
Rows 56 through 64: With Fisherman, rep Rows 8 through 16. At end of Row 64, cut Fisherman.
Rows 65, 66 and 67: With Brt. Watermelon, rep Rows 5, 6 and 7. At end of Row 67, cut Brt. Watermelon.
Row 68: With Orange, rep Row 8.
Rows 69 through 71: Rep Row 2, three times. At end of Row 71, finish off Orange. Weave in all ends.

crocheted
DIAGONAL
DIAMONDS

designed by Mary Thomas

Quick to make — 2 strands of yarn and a size K hook — a project sure to please any crocheter.

SIZE: Approx 48″ x 64″ before fringing

MATERIALS
Worsted weight yarn: 52 oz light peach
Size K aluminum crochet hook (or size required for gauge)
Materials Note: Two strands of yarn are used throughout patt.

GAUGE: With 2 strands of yarn in sc, 5 sts = 2″

INSTRUCTIONS

With 2 strands of yarn, ch 134 *loosely.*

Row 1: Sc in 2nd ch from hook and in each of next 4 chs; * ch 5, sk 3 chs, sc in each of next 5 chs; rep from * across.

Row 2: Ch 1, turn; sc in each of first 4 sc; * ch 3, sc in ch-5 sp; ch 3, sk one sc, sc in each of next 3 sc; rep from * across to last sc, sc in last sc.

Row 3: Ch 1, turn; sc in each of first 3 sc; * ch 3, sc in next ch-3 sp, sc in next sc (between ch-3 sps), sc in next ch-3 sp; ch 3, sk next sc, sc in next sc; rep from * across to last 2 sc, sc in each of last 2 sc.

Row 4: Ch 3, turn; sk first sc, dc in next sc; ch 3, sc in next ch-3 sp; sc in each of next 3 sc, sc in next ch-3 sp; * ch 5, sk next sc, sc in next ch-3 sp, sc in each of next 3 sc, sc in next ch-3 sp; rep from * to last 3 sc; ch 3, sk next sc, dc in each of last 2 sc.

Row 5: Ch 1, turn; sc in each of first 2 dc, sc in next ch-3 sp; * ch 3, sk one sc, sc in each of next 3 sc; ch 3, sc in next ch-5 sp; rep from * across, ending last rep by working sc in next ch-3 sp instead of ch-5 sp; sc in next dc, sc in top of ch-3.

Row 6: Ch 1, turn; sc in each of first 3 sc; * sc in next ch-3 sp, ch 3, sk one sc, sc in next sc; ch 3, sc in next ch-3 sp, sc in next sc; rep from * to last 2 sc, sc in each of last 2 sc.

Row 7: Ch 1, turn; sc in each of first 4 sc; * sc in next ch-3 sp, ch 5, sk next sc, sc in next ch-3 sp; sc in each of next 3 sc; rep from * to last sc, sc in last sc.

Rep Rows 2 through 7 until work measures approx 64″ long, ending by working Row 6.

Last Row: Ch 1, turn; sc in each of first 4 sc; * sc in next ch-3 sp, ch 3, sk next sc, sc in next ch-3 sp; sc in each of next 3 sc; rep from * to last sc, sc in last sc. Finish off; weave in all ends.

Fringe
Following *Fringe* instructions on pages 9 and 10, make triple knot fringe. Cut 25″ strands; use 8 strands for each knot of fringe. Tie knots evenly spaced (approx every 4th st) across each short end of afghan. Then work double and triple knots per instructions. Trim ends evenly.

crocheted
SUNSHINE

This bright lap robe, sure to keep your knees and legs warm, is quick and easy to make.

SIZE: Approx 34″ x 40″ before fringing

MATERIALS
Worsted weight yarn: 22 oz bright yellow
Size K aluminum crochet hook (or size required for gauge)

GAUGE: In sc, 5 sts = 2″

INSTRUCTIONS

Ch 100 *loosely*.

Row 1 (right side): Sc in 2nd ch from hook and in each rem ch across = 99 sc.

Row 2: Ch 2, turn; sk first 2 sc, 2 sc in next sc; * ch 1, sk 2 sc, 2 sc in next sc; rep from * across.

Row 3: Ch 2, turn; 2 hdc in each ch-1 sp across, ending 2 hdc in sp under Tch (turning chain).

Row 4: Ch 2, turn; 2 sc in sp between first two hdc groups, ch 1; * 2 sc in sp between next two hdc groups, ch 1; rep from * across, ending 2 sc in sp under Tch.

Rep Rows 3 and 4 until afghan measures approx 40″ long, ending by working Row 4.

Last Row: Ch 1, turn; sc in each sc and in each ch-1 sp across, ending sc in sp under Tch. Finish off; weave in all ends.

Fringe
Following *Fringe* instructions on page 9, make single knot fringe. Cut 12″ strands; use 3 strands for each knot of fringe. Tie one knot in every other sc across each short end of afghan.

crocheted worked-in design
AFGHAN, AFGHAN
designed by Carol Wilson Mansfield

A graphic contemporary design — ideal for the modern setting.

SIZE: Approx 43″ x 55″

MATERIALS
Worsted weight yarn: 28 oz caramel;
4 oz each black, brown, rust, medium beige, light beige and creme
Size H aluminum crochet hook (or size required for gauge)

GAUGE: In sc, 4 sts = 1″; 4 rows = 1″

INSTRUCTIONS

Note: On each row throughout patt (excluding edging), carry color not in use. [**To Carry Color: Place color not in use on top of row and work following sts over it (Fig 1 — color will be hidden inside of sts) = color carried.**]

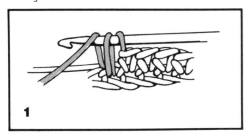

With caramel, ch 147 *loosely.*

Row 1 (right side): Continuing with caramel and carrying black across row, sc in 2nd ch from hook and in each rem ch across = 146 sc.

Note: At beg of each following row, bring color not in use up and in front of working strand **(Fig 2)**; then with working color, ch 1 and turn (color not in use will be inside of chain).

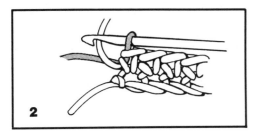

Row 2: Continuing with caramel and carrying black, ch 1, turn; sc in each sc across.

Row 3: Continuing with caramel and carrying black, ch 1, turn; sc in first sc; sc in next sc, changing to black [**To Change Colors: Work sc until 2 lps rem on hook; drop color being used but do not cut; with new color, YO and draw through 2 lps on hook (Fig 3) = color changed.**]; continuing with black and carrying caramel, sc in each sc to last 3 sc; sc in next sc, changing to caramel; continuing with caramel and carrying black, sc in each of last 2 sc.

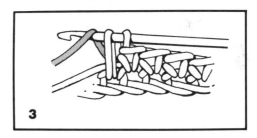

Row 4: Rep Row 3.

Rows 5 and 6: Rep Row 2, twice.

Row 7: Continuing with caramel and carrying black, ch 1, turn; sc in first sc; sc in next sc, changing to black; continuing with black and carrying caramel, sc in each of next 34 sc; † **sc in next sc, changing to caramel; continuing with caramel and carrying black, sc in each of next 2 sc; sc in next sc, changing to black; continuing with black and carrying caramel, sc in each of next 6 sc; sc in next sc, changing to caramel; continuing with caramel and carrying black, sc in next sc; sc in next sc, changing to black †** ; continuing with black and carrying caramel, sc in each of next 58 sc; rep from † to † once; continuing with black and carrying caramel, sc in each of next 23 sc; sc in next sc, changing to caramel; continuing with caramel and carrying black, sc in each of last 2 sc.

Fig 4

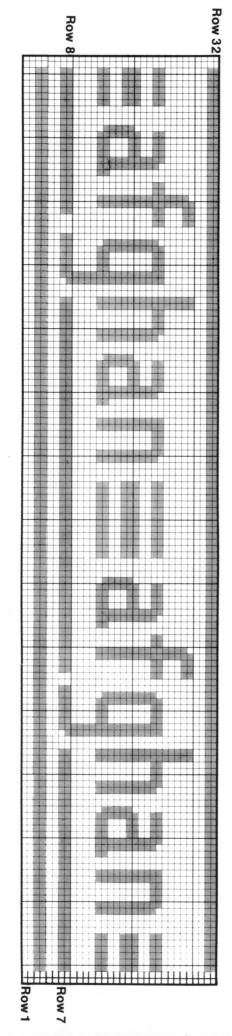

Now compare your work with chart in **Fig 4.** You have completed the first 7 rows. Working even in sc, continue working from chart, using black for the contrasting color. Beg with Row 8 and work through Row 32. Each square on chart represents one sc. On each odd-numbered row, work chart from right to left. On each even-numbered row, work chart from left to right. **Color Note:** Remember to change colors in sc before new color begins.

When 32 rows of chart have been completed, finish off black and begin carrying brown. Rep chart in **Fig 4,** 5 times more, working contrasting color of each 32-row repeat in the following color sequence: brown, rust, med beige, lt beige and creme.

When last 32-row repeat is completed, continuing with caramel and carrying creme, work 2 more rows even in sc. Finish off creme; continue with caramel and work edging.

Edging
[**Note:** *All rnds are worked on right side.*]

Rnd 1: Ch 3, turn. Across last row worked; (dc, ch 2, 2 dc) in first st for corner; * dc in each of next 3 sts, dc dec over next 2 sts [**To Work Dc Dec: Work dc in first st until 2 lps rem on hook; keeping the 2 lps on hook, YO, insert hook in next st and draw up a lp (4 lps now on hook); YO and draw through 2 lps; then YO and draw through rem 3 lps = dc dec made.**]; rep from * to last 5 sts, dc in each of next 4 sts, (2 dc, ch 2, 2 dc) in last st for corner. Across next edge (along end of rows); * dc in each of next 3 rows, dc dec over next 2 rows; rep from * to last 3 rows, dc in each of last 3 rows. Work rem 2 edges in same manner; join with a sl st in top of beg ch-3.

Rnd 2: Ch 3, do not turn; dc in each dc around and work (2 dc, ch 2, 2 dc) in each corner ch-2 sp; join with a sl st in top of beg ch-3.

Rnds 3 through 6: Rep Rnd 2, four times.

Finish off; weave in all ends. Lightly steam press on wrong side.

☐ **caramel**
▦ **contrasting color**

crocheted
SIX-POINTED STAR

This afghan is worked mostly in diamond shaped motifs, which are then joined to form a star pattern, one of the most popular quilt designs of all time.

SIZE: Approx 46″ x 62″

MATERIALS
Worsted weight yarn: 24 oz shaded browns ombre;
20 oz medium brown;
2 oz ecru (for edging only)

GAUGE: In dc, 13 sts = 4″

DIAMOND MOTIF INSTRUCTIONS
Row 1: Ch 4, 2 dc in 4th ch from hook = 3 dc [**Note:** *Ch-3 counts as one dc throughout patt.*]

Row 2: Ch 3, turn; dc in first dc (inc made), dc in next dc, 2 dc in top of ch-3 [**Note:** *Turning ch (ch-3) will be called a dc from here on.*] = 5 dc.

Row 3: Ch 3, turn; dc in first dc (inc made); dc in each dc to last dc, 2 dc in last dc = 7 dc.

Rows 4 and 5: Rep Row 3, twice. At end of Row 5, you should have 11 dc.

Row 6: Ch 3, turn; sk first dc, dc in each rem dc across = 11 dc.

Row 7: Ch 3, turn; sk first dc, work dec over next 2 dc [**To Work Dec: (YO, insert hook in next st and draw up a lp; YO and draw through 2 lps on hook) twice; YO and draw through all 3 lps on hook = dec made.**]; dc in each dc to last 3 dc; dec over next 2 dc, dc in last dc = 9 dc.

Rows 8 and 9: Rep Row 7, twice. At end of Row 9, you should have 5 dc.

Row 10: Ch 3, turn; sk first dc; keeping last lp of each st on hook, dc in each of next 4 dc (5 lps now on hook); YO and draw through all 5 lps on hook. Finish off.

AFGHAN INSTRUCTIONS

Star Hexagon (make 18)
Following prev *Diamond Motif Instructions,* make 6 motifs with ombre and 6 motifs with brown (12 total).

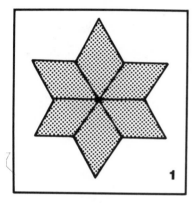

First, sew 6 ombre motifs tog in star form as shown in **Fig 1,** keeping Row 1 of each motif at center. Be sure to match rows carefully. Next, add brown motifs as shown in **Fig 2** and sew in place. Lightly steam press on wrong side.

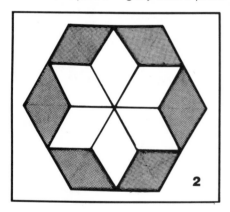

Half Hexagon (make 4)
Following *Diamond Motif Instructions,* make 3 motifs with ombre and 2 motifs with brown (5 total). Then with brown, make 2 Triangle Motifs by working (Rows 1 through 5 of *Diamond Motif Instructions;* finish off) twice.

Refer to **Fig 3** and join motifs tog as follows. First, sew 3 ombre motifs tog for half of star; then add 2 brown diamond-shaped motifs, and lastly one triangle at each side. Lightly steam press on wrong side.

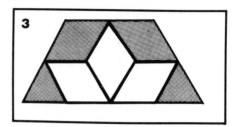

Assembling
Refer to diagram in **Fig 4** for placement, and sew Star Hexagons and Half Hexagons tog. [**Note:** *There are 2 Half Hexagons at top edge and 2 Half Hexagons at bottom edge which have been indicated by arrows.*] Then with brown, make 9 Diamond Motifs (D) and 2 Triangle Motifs (T) and sew in place along side edges as indicated in Fig 4.

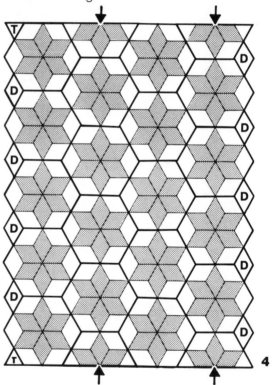

Edging
With right side facing, join ecru with a sl st in any corner of afghan. **Rnd 1:** Ch 1, work in sc evenly spaced around afghan (working 3 sc at each outer corner), join with a sl st in beg sc. **Rnd 2:** Do not turn; working from **left to right** in reverse sc **(see Figs 5 and 6),** work one st in each st around. Finish off; weave in all ends. Lightly steam press joinings on wrong side.

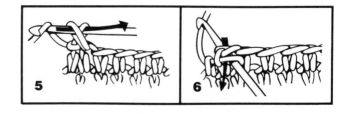

crocheted quilt
LOG CABIN

designed by Doris England

Inspired by one of the most common quilt patterns of the early Colonial days, this design is sure to be a family heirloom.

SIZE: Approx 54″ x 76″

MATERIALS
Sport weight yarn: 8 oz rust;
8 oz light gray;
8 oz dark gray;
8 oz beige;
9 oz camel;
13 oz dark brown;
11 oz off white
Size H aluminum crochet hook (or size required for gauge)

GAUGE: One square = 12″

INSTRUCTIONS
Square (make 24)
[**Note:** *Refer to* **Fig 1** *for construction and color scheme of square.*]

Center: With rust, ch 15. **Row 1:** Sc in 3rd ch from hook; (ch 1, sk one ch, sc in next ch) 6 times. **Row 2:** Ch 2, turn; sc in first ch-1 sp; (ch 1, sc in next ch-1 sp) 5 times; ch 1, sc in sp under ch-2 at end of row. **Rows 3 through 14:** Rep Row 2, 12 times. At end of Row 14, change to lt gray in last sc. [**To Change Colors: Work last sc of row until 2 lps rem on hook; leaving 4″ ends for weaving in now or later, finish off color being used; with new color, YO and draw through 2 lps on hook = color changed.**]

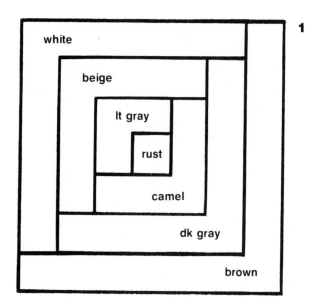

1

Lt Gray Band: Row 1: Ch 2, turn; working back across row just worked, sc in first ch-1 sp; (ch 1, sc in next ch-1 sp) 5 times; ch 1, work (sc, ch 2, sc) in ch-2 sp at end of row for corner; continuing across side edge of rust center, work (ch 1, sk next row, sc in next row) 6 times; ch 1, sk last row, sc in beg ch of foundation chain.

Row 2: Ch 2, turn; work (sc, ch 1) in each ch-1 sp to ch-2 corner sp; work (sc, ch 2, sc) in corner sp; work (ch 1, sc) in each rem ch-1 sp, ending ch 1, sc in sp under Tch (turning chain). **Rows 3 through 7:** Rep Row 2, five times.
At end of Row 7, change to camel in last sc.

Camel Band: Row 1: Ch 2, do not turn; working across end of lt gray band and beg row of rust center, (sc in next row, ch 1, sk next row) 3 times; sc in first sc of rust center; (ch 1, sc in next ch-1 sp) 6 times; ch 1, work (sc, ch 2, sc) in ch-2 sp at corner; working across side edge of rust center and end of lt gray band, (ch 1, sc in next row, sk next row) 6 times; (ch 1, sc in next row) twice [row of each color]; (ch 1, sk next row, sc in next row) 3 times.

Rows 2 through 7: Rep Rows 2 through 7 of Lt Gray Band. At end of Row 7, change to beige in last sc.

Beige Band: [**Note:** *On first row, you will be working across ends of Camel Band and last row of Lt Gray band.*] **Row 1:** Ch 2, do not turn; (sc in next row, ch 1, sk next row) 3 times; ch 1, sc in Tch sp at beg of next color band; work (ch 1, sc in next ch-1 sp) in each ch-1 sp to corner; ch 1, work (sc, ch 2, sc) in corner sp; work (ch 1, sc in next ch-1 sp) in each ch-1 sp to beg of next color band; ch 1, sc in first row (at end of next color band); (ch 1, sk next row, sc in next row) 3 times.

Rows 2 through 7: Rep Rows 2 through 7 of Lt Gray Band. At end of Row 7, change to dk gray in last sc.

Dk Gray Band: [**Note:** *On first row, you will be working across ends of Beige Band and last row of Camel Band.*] Work same as Beige Band. At end of last row, change to white in last sc.

White Band: [**Note:** *On first row, you will be working across ends of Dk Gray Band and last row of Beige Band.*] Work same as Beige Band. At end of last row, change to brown in last sc.

Brown Band: [**Note:** *On first row, you will be working across ends of White Band and last row of Dk Gray Band.*] Work same as Beige Band. At end of last row, finish off; weave in all ends.

Assembling

Arrange squares as shown in **Fig 2.** Be sure to have last row of each square facing up for right side of afghan. To join, hold two squares with right sides tog. Using matching yarn, beg in ch st at corner and sew across (carefully matching sts), ending in ch st at next corner. Join squares in rows; then sew rows tog in same manner, being sure to firmly join each four-corner junction.

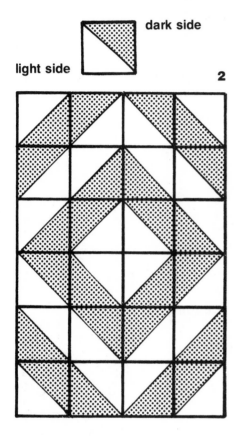

light side / dark side

2

Border

With right side facing, join camel with a sl st in any outer corner sp of afghan.

Rnd 1: Ch 1, work (sc, ch 2, sc, ch 1) in same sp; work (sc, ch 1) in each ch sp of squares and in every other row across ends of brown bands around afghan; and in each rem corner sp, work (sc, ch 2, sc, ch 1); join with a sl st in beg sc.

Rnd 2: Ch 1, turn; sl st into ch-1 sp, ch 1; sc in same sp, ch 1; work (sc, ch 1) in each ch-1 sp around; and in each corner sp, work (sc, ch 2, sc, ch 1); join with a sl st in beg sc.

Rnds 3 through 5: Rep Rnd 2, three times. At end of Rnd 5, finish off camel.

Rnd 6: Turn; join rust with a sl st in any corner sp; ch 1, (sc, ch 2, sc, ch 1) in same sp; complete rnd in same manner as Rnd 2.

Rnds 7 through 13: Rep Rnd 2, seven times. At end of Rnd 13, finish off rust.

Rnd 14: With lt gray, rep Rnd 6.

Rnds 15 and 16: Rep Rnd 2, twice. At end of Rnd 16, finish off; weave in all ends. Lightly steam press joinings on wrong side.

crocheted
WILLIAMSBURG
designed by Jean Leinhauser

SIZE: Approx 52" x 61"

MATERIALS
Worsted weight yarn: 8 oz medium blue;
16 oz dark blue;
12 oz ecru;
16 oz camel;
18 oz dark brown
Size J aluminum crochet hook (or size required for gauge)

GAUGE: One square = 9½"

INSTRUCTIONS

Square (make 35)
[**Note:** *All rnds are worked on right side.*]

With med blue, ch 6, join with a sl st to form a ring.

Rnd 1: Work beg PC (popcorn) in ring [**To Work Beg PC: Ch 3, 3 dc in ring or sp; drop lp from hook, insert hook in top of beg ch-3; hook dropped lp and pull through st (Fig 1), ch 1 tightly = beg PC made.**]; * ch 3, work PC in ring [**To Work PC: 4 dc in ring or sp; drop lp from hook, insert hook in first dc of 4-dc group just made; hook dropped lp and pull through st, ch 1 tightly = PC made.**]; rep from * twice more, ch 3, join with a sl st in top of ch-3 of beg PC. Finish off.

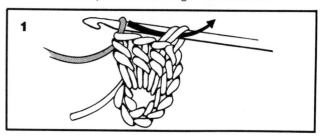

Rnd 2: With right side facing, join camel with a sl st in any ch-3 sp; work (beg PC, ch 3, PC) in same sp as joining, ch 3; * work (PC, ch 3, PC) in next ch-3 sp, ch 3; rep from * twice more, join with a sl st in top of ch-3 of beg PC. Finish off.

Rnd 3: With right side facing, join dk blue with a sl st in any ch-3 sp between pair of PCs worked into same sp; ch 3, 2 dc in same sp, ch 1; work (3 dc, ch 2, 3 dc) in next ch-3 sp for corner; * ch 1, 3 dc in next sp (between pair of PCs worked into same sp), ch 1; work (3 dc, ch 2, 3 dc) in next sp for corner; rep from * twice more, ch 1, join with a sl st in top of beg ch-3. Finish off.

Rnd 4: With right side facing, join med blue with a sl st in any corner ch-2 sp; ch 3, (2 dc, ch 2, 3 dc) in same sp; * work (ch 1, 3 dc) in each ch-1 sp along side to corner, ch 1; work (3 dc, ch 2, 3 dc) in corner ch-2 sp; rep from * twice more; work (ch 1, 3 dc) in each ch-1 sp along last side, ch 1, join with a sl st in top of beg ch-3. Finish off.

Rnd 5: With dk blue, rep Rnd 4.

Rnd 6: With ecru, rep Rnd 4.

Rnd 7: With camel, rep Rnd 4.

Rnd 8: With brown, rep Rnd 4. Finish off; weave in all ends.

Assembling
Afghan is 5 squares wide by 7 squares long. To join, hold two squares with right sides tog. Thread tapestry needle with brown. Working in **back (outer) lps only (Fig 2),** sew squares tog along one side, carefully matching sts and corner sps. Continue joining squares into rows; then sew rows tog, being sure that each four-corner junction is firmly joined.

Border
With right side facing you, join brown with a sl st in any ch-2 corner sp of afghan. Working in same manner as Rnd 4 of Square, work one rnd in each of the following colors: brown, ecru, med blue and dk blue. When all 4 rnds of border have been completed, finish off and weave in all loose ends.

Knits in Squares and Strips

The following four afghans represent a special technique developed by Joan Harmon of Glen Ellyn, Illinois.

Joan, an avid knitter, was aware of the popularity of granny squares for crocheters — but could find nothing similar for knitters. After months of research, she was unable to uncover any satisfactory techniques for making good knitted square designs; so she began designing her own. Joan's squares are worked on five double pointed needles (that may sound difficult, but it isn't), and her cornering methods are unique. She now publishes these patterns under the name of *Squariginals.*

We like Joan's technique for knitted squares so much that we asked her to let us include some of her designs in this book. All of her designs and techniques are copyrighted by her, and are used here with her permission.

Before starting any of these four beautiful afghans, be sure to read the *Special Techniques* section which follows.

SPECIAL TECHNIQUES

To work a square in knitting, you will be working in rounds on five double pointed needles. Stitches are distributed evenly onto four needles (one needle for each side of square), with the fifth needle free (for knitting the stitches off the next needle).

For ease in starting, we recommend beginning with three needles instead of four — stitches for one side on the first needle, stitches for the next side on the second needle, and stitches for the other two sides on the third needle **(Fig 1).**

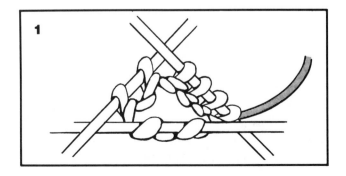

After working several rounds or when stitches become too crowded on the third needle (stitches for two sides of the square), slip the stitches for one side (half the number of stitches on needle) onto the extra (fourth) needle.

To work a YO at the beginning of a round, bring yarn to front of work and then over the needle before knitting the first stitch **(Fig 2).**

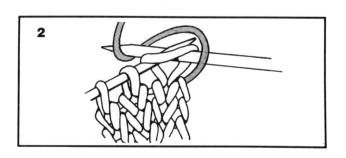

knitted squares
PUFFPETAL

designed and © by Joan Harmon

This pattern is made in squares of a charming flower design. The squares are knitted with five double pointed needles. Before beginning your afghan, read *Special Techniques* on page 67.

SIZE: Approx 49″ x 63″

MATERIALS
Worsted weight yarn: **12 oz cream;**
                           16 oz rust;
                           20 oz dark green
Size 10, five double pointed needles (or size required for gauge)
Cable needle
Stitch marker

GAUGE: One square = 7″

INSTRUCTIONS

Square
(Make 63 total: 15 cream, 20 rust and 28 green)

Leaving 2″ yarn tail, CO 8 sts onto one needle; then divide sts onto 3 needles as follows: 2-2-4. Join, being careful not to twist sts. [**Note:** *Fourth needle is used later (see Special Techniques on page 67)*].

Rnd 1: (YO, K1) 8 times = 16 sts (4 sts each side of square). [**Note:** Place marker for end of rnd; move marker on each following rnd.]

Rnd 2: * K1, P1, K2; rep from * 3 times more.

Rnd 3: * K1, YO; sl 1 as to purl (now and throughout patt), YO, K1; K1 with 2 wraps [**To Work K1 With 2 Wraps: Insert needle into next st as to knit, wrap yarn twice around tip of right-hand needle; now knit this st, carrying extra wraps on right-hand needle = K1 with 2 wraps.**]; rep from * 3 times more.

Rnd 4: * K2, P1, K2; knit next st, dropping extra wraps; rep from * 3 times more = 24 sts (6 sts each side).

Rnd 5: * K1, (sl 1, YO) twice; sl 1, K1; K1 with 2 wraps; rep from * 3 times more.

Rnd 6: * K3, P1, K3; knit next st, dropping extra wraps; rep from * 3 times more = 32 sts (8 sts each side).

Rnd 7: * K2; (sl 1, YO) twice; sl 1, K2; K1 with 2 wraps; rep from * 3 times more.

Rnd 8: * K4, P1, K4; knit next st, dropping extra wraps; rep from * 3 times more = 40 sts (10 sts each side).

Rnd 9: * K3; (sl 1, YO) twice; sl 1, K3; K1 with 2 wraps; rep from * 3 times more.

Rnd 10: * K5, P1, K5; knit next st, dropping extra wraps; rep from * 3 times more = 48 sts (12 sts each side).

Rnd 11: * K4; (sl 1, YO) twice; sl 1, K4; K1 with 2 wraps; rep from * 3 times more.

Rnd 12: Front cross (abbreviated FC) [**To Work FC: Sl next st onto cable needle and hold at front of work; purl next st, then K1 from cable needle = FC made.**]; K4, P1, K4; back cross (abbreviated BC) [**To Work BC: Sl next st onto cable needle and hold at back of work; knit next st, then P1 from cable needle = BC made.**]; knit next st, dropping extra wraps; rep from * 3 times more = 56 sts (14 sts each side).

Rnd 13: * P1, FC, K2; (sl 1, YO) twice; sl 1, K2; BC, P1; K1 with 2 wraps; rep from * 3 times more.

Rnd 14: * P2, FC; K3, P1, K3; BC, P2; knit next st, dropping extra wraps; rep from * 3 times more = 64 sts (16 sts each side).

Rnd 15: * P3, FC, K1; (sl 1, YO) twice; sl 1, K1; BC, P3; K1 with 2 wraps; rep from * 3 times more.

Rnd 16: * P4, FC; K2, P1, K2; BC, P4; knit next st, dropping extra wraps; rep from * 3 times more = 72 sts (18 sts each side).

Rnd 17: * P5, FC; sl 3, BC, P5; K1 with 2 wraps; rep from * 3 times more.

Rnd 18: * YO, P6, FC; P1, BC, P6; YO twice; knit next st, dropping extra wraps; rep from * 3 times more.

Rnd 19: * YO, P1; YO, P7; bring yarn to back of work, sl 1, K2 tog, PSSO; P7, YO, P1; drop next YO (extra YO of prev rnd); YO twice, P1; rep from * 3 times more.

Rnd 20: * K 21, drop extra YO, K1; rep from * 3 times more = 88 sts (22 sts each side).

Rnd 21: * YO twice; K2, YO, K8, sl 1, K8; YO, K2; YO, K1; rep from * 3 times more.

Rnd 22: * P1, drop extra YO, P 25; rep from * 3 times more = 104 sts (26 sts each side).

BO all sts *loosely* in knit, leaving 12″ yarn end; thread into tapestry needle. Insert needle through first st bound off; then through last st bound off and secure for a neat closing of square. Thread center yarn tail into tapestry needle; secure to first and last CO sts. Weave in remaining yarn ends.

Assembling
Position squares (with right sides facing up) as shown in **Fig 1.** To join, hold two squares side by side. Loosely whipstitch squares tog, working through both lps of each corresponding st across side. Join squares into rows; then join rows tog, being sure to have each four-corner junction securely joined. Weave in all yarn ends. Lightly steam press joinings on wrong side.

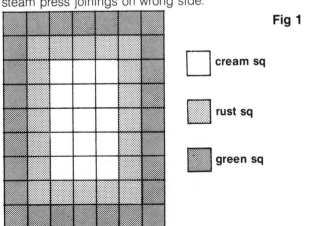

Fig 1

☐ cream sq

▨ rust sq

▦ green sq

knitted squares
STARFLOWER
designed and © by Joan Harmon

Before beginning your afghan, read *Special Techniques* on page 67.

SIZE: Approx 48″ x 72″

MATERIALS
Worsted weight yarn: 36 oz white;
12 oz black
Size 10½, five double pointed needles (or size required for gauge)
Size H aluminum crochet hook (for edging only)
Stitch marker

GAUGE: One square = 8″

INSTRUCTIONS

Square (make 54)

With white, leaving 2″ yarn tail, CO 8 sts onto one needle; then divide sts onto 3 needles as follows: 2-2-4. Join, being careful not to twist sts. [**Note:** *Fourth needle is used later (see Special Techniques on page 67).*]

Rnd 1: (YO, K1) 8 times = 16 sts (4 sts each side of square). [**Note:** *Place marker for end of rnd; move marker on each following rnd.*]

Rnd 2: * K1, sl 1 as to purl, K2; rep from * 3 times more.

Rnd 3: * YO, K3, YO, K1; rep from * 3 times more = 24 sts (6 sts each side).

Rnd 4: Knit.

Rnd 5: * YO, K5, YO, K1; rep from * 3 times more = 32 sts (8 sts each side).

Rnd 6: Knit.

Rnd 7: * YO, K7, YO, K1; rep from * 3 times more = 40 sts (10 sts each side).

Rnd 8: Knit.

Rnd 9: * YO, K9, YO, K1; rep from * 3 times more = 48 sts (12 sts each side).

Rnd 10: * YO, K 11, YO, K1; rep from * 3 times more = 56 sts (14 sts each side).

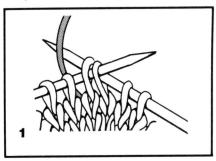

Rnd 11: * YO, work a single dec over next 2 sts [**To Work Single Dec: Sl first st as to knit, sl second st as to purl; insert tip of left-hand needle into these same 2 sts (Fig 1) and K2 tog in this position = single dec made.**]; YO, K3; work a double dec over next 3 sts [**To Work Double Dec: Sl 1 as to purl, K2 tog, PSSO = double dec made.**]; K3, YO, K2 tog; YO, K1; rep from * 3 times more = 56 sts (14 sts each side).

Rnd 12: * K6, sl 1 as to purl, K7; rep from * 3 times more.

Rnd 13: * YO, K1, YO; work a single dec over next 2 sts (same as in Rnd 11); YO, K2; work a double dec over next 3 sts (same as in Rnd 11); K2, YO, K2 tog; (YO, K1) twice; rep from * 3 times more = 64 sts (16 sts each side).

Rnd 14: * K7, sl 1 as to purl, K8; rep from * 3 times more.

Rnd 15: * YO, K1; (YO, work a single dec over next 2 sts) twice; YO, K1; work a double dec over next 3 sts; K1, (YO, K2 tog) twice; (YO, K1) twice; rep from * 3 times more = 72 sts (18 sts each side).

Rnd 16: * K8, sl 1 as to purl, K9; rep from * 3 times more.

Rnd 17: * YO, K1; (YO, work a single dec over next 2 sts) 3 times; YO, work a double dec over next 3 sts; (YO, K2 tog) 3 times; (YO, K1) twice; rep from * 3 times more = 80 sts (20 sts each side).

Rnd 18: Drop white (do not cut); join black and knit around.

Rnd 19: With black, * YO, P1; (YO, P2 tog) 4 times; YO, P1; (YO, P2 tog) 4 times; YO, P1; YO, K1; rep from * 3 times more = 96 sts (24 sts each side).

Rnd 20: With black, knit. At end of rnd, finish off black.

Rnd 21: Continuing with white only, * YO; (K1, P1) 11 times; K1, YO, K1; rep from * 3 times more = 104 sts (26 sts each side).

Rnd 22: * (K1, P1) 12 times, K2; rep from * 3 times more.

BO all sts *loosely* in knit, leaving 12" yarn end; thread into tapestry needle. Insert needle through first st bound off; then through last st bound off and secure for a neat closing of square. Thread center yarn tail into tapestry needle; secure to first and last CO sts. Weave in remaining yarn ends.

Assembling
Afghan is 6 squares wide by 9 squares long. To join, hold two squares side by side. Thread white into a tapestry needle. Loosely whipstitch squares tog across side, carefully matching sts. Join squares into rows; then join rows tog, being sure to have each four-corner junction securely joined.

Edging
With right side facing, use crochet hook and black and work one rnd in sc evenly spaced (approx one st in each st and in each joining; and 3 sc in each corner) around afghan. Weave in ends. Lightly steam press joinings on wrong side.

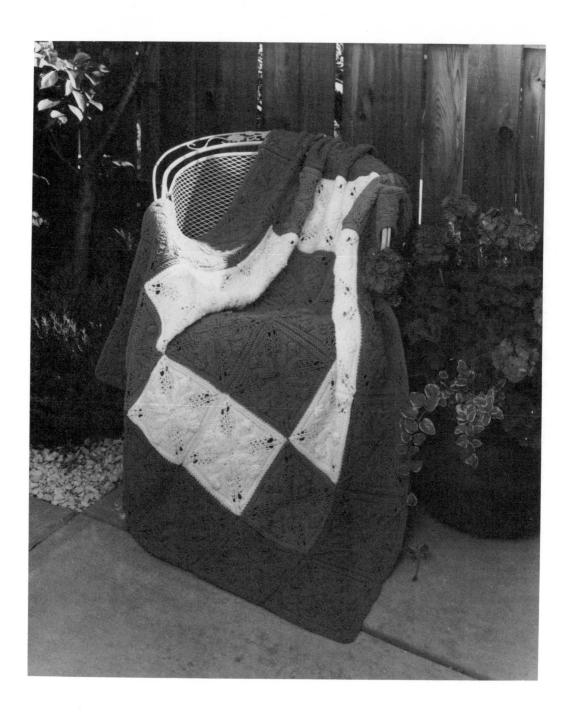

knitted squares
GERANIUM

designed and © by Joan Harmon

Bright and cheerful spring colors highlight this lovely afghan — made in squares which are knitted with five double pointed needles. Before beginning your afghan, read *Special Techniques* on page 67.

SIZE: Approx 48″ x 56″

MATERIALS
Worsted weight yarn: 10 oz white;
10 oz geranium;
20 oz spring green
Size 10½, five double pointed needles (or size required for gauge)
Cable needle
Stitch marker

GAUGE: One square = 8″

INSTRUCTIONS

Square
(Make 42 total: 10 white, 10 geranium and 22 green)

Leaving 2″ yarn tail, CO 8 sts onto one needle; then divide sts onto 3 needles as follows: 2-2-4. Join, being careful not twist sts. [**Note:** *Fourth needle is used later (see Special Techniques on page 67).*]

Rnd 1: (YO, K1) 8 times = 16 sts (4 sts each side of square). [**Note:** *Place marker for end of rnd; move marker on each following rnd.*]

Rnd 2: Purl.

Rnd 3: * P1; (K1, YO, K1) all next st, P2; rep from * 3 times more = 24 sts (6 sts each side).

Rnd 4: * P1, K1; sl 1 as to purl (now and throughout patt), K1, P2; rep from * 3 times more.

Rnd 5: * P1, K1; (K1, YO, K1) all in next st; K1, P2; rep from * 3 times more = 32 sts (8 sts each side).

Rnd 6: * P1, K2; sl 1, K2, P2; rep from * 3 times more.

Rnd 7: * P1, K2; (K1, YO, K1) all in next st; K2, P1, YO, P1; rep from * 3 times more = 44 sts (11 sts each side).

Rnd 8: * P1, K3; sl 1, K3, P1; drop next st (YO of prev rnd); YO, P1; rep from * 3 times more = 44 sts (11 sts each side).

Rnd 9: * P1, K3; (K1, YO, K1) all in next st; K3, P1; drop next st (YO of prev rnd); YO, P1; rep from * 3 times more = 52 sts (13 sts each side).

Rnd 10: * P1, K3, P1; sl 1, P1; K3, P1; drop next st (YO of prev rnd); YO, P1; rep from * 3 times more = 52 sts (13 sts each side).

Rnd 11: * (K1, P1) all in next st; K3, P1, K1; P1, K3; (P1, K1) all in next st; drop next st (YO of prev rnd); YO, K1; rep from * 3 times more = 60 sts (15 sts each side).

Rnd 12: * P3, K2, P1; sl 1, P1; K2, P3; drop next st (YO of prev rnd); YO, K1; rep from * 3 times more = 60 sts (15 sts each side).

Rnd 13: * (K1, P1) all in next st, P1; sl next st onto cable needle and hold at back of work; knit next 2 sts, then P1 from cable needle; P1, K1, P1; sl next 2 sts onto cable needle and hold at front of work; purl next st, then K2 from cable needle; P1, (P1, K1) all in next st; drop next st (YO of prev rnd); YO, K1; rep from * 3 times more = 68 sts (17 sts each side).

Rnd 14: * P3; sl next st onto cable needle and hold at back of work; knit next st, then K1 from cable needle; P2, sl 1, P2; sl next st onto cable needle and hold at front of work; knit next st, then K1 from cable needle; P3, drop next st (YO of prev rnd); YO, K1; rep from * 3 times more = 68 sts (17 sts each side).

Rnd 15: * (K1, P1) all in next st, P1; sl next st onto cable needle and hold at back of work; knit next st, then K1 from cable needle; P2, work (K1, return this st to left needle and reknit st again) in each of the next 3 sts; P2, sl next st onto cable needle and hold at front of work; knit next st, then K1 from cable needle; P1, (P1, K1) all in next st; drop next st (YO of prev rnd); YO, K1; rep from * 3 times more = 76 sts (19 sts each side).

Rnd 16: * P7; work (K1, P1, K1) into each of the next 3 sts (9 sts total); P7, drop next st (YO of prev rnd); YO, K1; rep from * 3 times more = 100 sts (25 sts each side).

Rnd 17: * (K1, P1) all in next st, P6; work (knit next 3 sts, return these 3 sts to left needle; bring yarn to front of work and purl these 3 sts tog) 3 times; P6, (P1, K1) all in next st; drop next st (YO of prev rnd); YO, K1; rep from * 3 times more = 84 sts (21 sts each side).

Rnd 18: * YO, P8, K3 tog through back loops; P8, drop next st (YO of prev rnd); YO, K1; rep from * 3 times more = 80 sts (20 sts each side).

Rnd 19: * YO, K1, YO; K8, sl 1, K8; YO, K1; YO twice, K1; rep from * 3 times more.

Rnd 20: * K23, drop extra YO, K1; rep from * 3 times more = 96 sts (24 sts each side).

Rnd 21: * YO, P 23; YO twice, K1; rep from * 3 times more.

Rnd 22: * P 25, drop extra YO, K1; rep from * 3 times more = 104 sts (26 sts each side).

BO all sts *loosely* in knit, leaving 12″ yarn end. Thread into tapestry needle; insert through first st bound off; then through last st bound off and secure for a neat closing of square. Thread center yarn tail into tapestry needle; secure to first and last CO sts. Weave in remaining yarn ends.

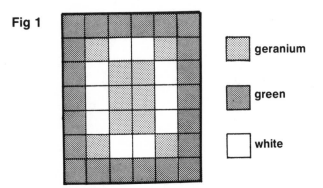

Fig 1

geranium

green

white

Assembling
Position squares (with right sides facing up) as shown in **Fig 1**. To join, hold two squares side by side. Loosely whipstitch squares tog, working through both lps of each corresponding st across side. Join squares into rows; then join rows tog, being sure to have each four-corner junction securely joined. Weave in all yarn ends. Lightly steam press joinings on wrong side.

knitted squares
CHOCOLATE MEDALLION
designed and © by Joan Harmon

Squares — knitted with five needles — are sewn together diagonally to form this innovative design. Half squares — added along the edges — are worked in rows on two needles only. Before beginning your afghan, read *Special Techniques* on page 67.

SIZE: Approx 46″ x 70″

MATERIALS
Worsted weight yarn: 30 oz light yellow;
8 oz brown
Size 10½, five double pointed needles (or size required for gauge)
Size G aluminum crochet hook (for edging only)
Stitch marker

GAUGE: One square = 8″

INSTRUCTIONS

Full Square
(Make 39 total: 30 yellow and 9 brown)

Leaving 2″ yarn tail, CO 8 sts onto one needle; then divide sts onto 3 needles as follows: 2-2-4. Join, being careful not to twist sts. [**Note:** *Fourth needle is used later (see Special Techniques on page 67).*]

Rnd 1: (YO, K1) 8 times = 16 sts (4 sts each side of square). [**Note:** *Place marker for end of rnd; move marker on each following rnd.*]

Rnd 2: * K1, P1, K2; rep from * 3 times more.

Rnd 3: * YO, K1; P1, K1; YO, K1; rep from * 3 times more = 24 sts (6 sts each side).

Rnd 4: * K2, sl 1 as to purl (now and throughout patt), K3; rep from * 3 times more.

Rnd 5: * YO, K2; P1, K2; YO, K1; rep from * 3 times more = 32 sts (8 sts each side).

Rnd 6: * K3, sl 1, K4; rep from * 3 times more.

Rnd 7: * YO, K3; P1, K3; YO, K1; rep from * 3 times more = 40 sts (10 sts each side).

Rnd 8: * K4, sl 1, K5; rep from * 3 times more.

Rnd 9: * YO, K4; P1, K4; YO, K1; rep from * 3 times more = 48 sts (12 sts each side).

Rnd 10: * K5, sl 1, K6; rep from * 3 times more.

Rnd 11: * YO, K2 tog; K2, sl 1; YO, P1, YO; sl 1, K2; work a dec over next 2 sts [**To Work Dec: Sl first st as to knit, sl second st as to purl; insert tip of left-hand needle into these same 2 sts (Fig 1) and K2 tog in this position = dec made.**]; YO twice, K1; rep from * 3 times more.

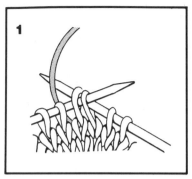

Rnd 12: * P1, K4; drop YO, sl 1, drop YO; K4, P1, drop extra YO, K1; rep from * 3 times more = 48 sts (12 sts each side).

Rnd 13: * YO, P1; YO, K2 tog; K2, (K1, P1, K1) all in next st, K2; work a dec over next 2 sts (same as in Rnd 11); YO, P1; YO twice, K1; rep from * 3 times more.

Rnd 14: * P3, K3; P1, sl 1, P1; K3, P3; drop extra YO, K1; rep from * 3 times more = 64 sts (16 sts each side).

Rnd 15: * YO, P3; YO, K2 tog; K1, P1; bring yarn to back of work, sl 1; bring yarn to front of work, P1; K1, work a dec over next 2 sts; YO, P3; YO twice, K1; rep from * 3 times more.

Rnd 16: * P5, K2; P3, K2; P5, drop extra YO, K1; rep from * 3 times more = 72 sts (18 sts each side).

Rnd 17: * YO, P5; YO, K2 tog; sl 1, P1; bring yarn to back of work, sl 1; work a dec over next 2 sts; YO, P5; YO twice, K1; rep from * 3 times more.

Rnd 18: * P 19, drop extra YO, K1; rep from * 3 times more = 80 sts (20 sts each side).

Rnd 19: * (YO, P2 tog) 4 times; YO, P3 tog; (YO, P2 tog) 4 times; YO twice, K1; rep from * 3 times more.

Rnd 20: * K 19, drop extra YO, K1; rep from * 3 times more = 80 sts (20 sts each side).

Rnd 21: * YO, K 19, YO; (P1, K1, P1) all into next st; rep from * 3 times more = 96 sts (24 sts each side).

Rnd 22: * P 22, K1, P1; rep from * 3 times more.

Beg with last st of prev rnd (sl st onto free needle), BO all sts in knit, leaving 12″ yarn end. Thread into tapestry needle; weave through first bound-off st, then through last bound-off st and secure for a neat closing of square. Thread center tail into tapestry needle; secure to first and last CO sts. Weave in remaining yarn ends.

Half Squares (make 16)

With yellow, CO 5 sts onto one needle. [**Note:** *You will be working back and forth in rows with 2 needles only.*]

Row 1 (right side): K1; (YO, K1) 4 times = 9 sts.

Row 2: P2, K1; P3, K1, P2.

Row 3: K1; * YO, K1, P1, K1; YO, K1; rep from * once more = 13 sts.

Row 4: P1; * P2, sl 1 as to purl (now and throughout patt), P3; rep from * once more.

Row 5: K1; * YO, K2; P1, K2; YO, K1; rep from * once more = 17 sts.

Row 6: P1; * P3, sl 1, P4; rep from * once more.

Row 7: K1; * YO, K3; P1, K3; YO, K1; rep from * once more = 21 sts.

Row 8: P1; * P4, sl 1, P5; rep from * once more.

Row 9: K1; * YO, K4; P1, K4; YO, K1; rep from * once more = 25 sts.

Row 10: P1; * P5, sl 1, P6; rep from * once more.

Row 11: K1; * YO, K2 tog; K2, sl 1; YO, P1, YO; sl 1, K2, work a dec over next 2 sts (same as in Rnd 11 of Full Square); YO twice, K1; rep from * once more.

Row 12: P1; * K1, drop extra YO; P4, drop YO; sl 1, drop YO; P4, K1, P1; rep from * once more = 25 sts.

Row 13: K1; * YO, P1; YO, K2 tog; K2, (K1, P1, K1) all in next st; K2, work a dec over next 2 sts (same as in Rnd 11 of Full Square); YO, P1; YO twice, K1; rep from * once more.

Row 14: P1; * K1, drop extra YO; K2, P3; K1, bring yarn toward you, sl 1; K1, P3, K3, P1; rep from * once more = 33 sts.

Row 15: K1; * YO, P3; YO, K2 tog; K1, P1; yarn to back of work, sl 1; P1, K1; work a dec over next 2 sts (same as in Rnd 11 of Full Square); YO, P3; YO twice, K1; rep from * once more.

Row 16: P1; * K1, drop extra YO; K4, P2; K3, P2; K5, P1; rep from * once more = 37 sts.

Row 17: K1; * YO, P5; YO, K2 tog; sl 1, P1, yarn to back of work, sl 1; work a dec over next 2 sts (same as in Rnd 11 of Full Square); YO, P5; YO twice, K1; rep from * once more.

Row 18: P1; * K1, drop extra YO; K18, P1; rep from * once more = 41 sts.

Row 19: K1; * (YO, P2 tog) 4 times; YO, P3 tog; (YO, P2 tog) 4 times, YO twice, K1; rep from * once more.

Row 20: P1; * P1, drop extra YO, P 19; rep from * once more = 41 sts.

Row 21: (P1, K1) all in next st; YO, P 19, YO; (P1, K1, P1) all in next st; YO, P 19; YO, (K1, P1) all in next st.

Row 22: K1, P1, K 22; P1, K 22; P1, K 1 = 49 sts. BO all sts *loosely* in knit. Weave in all ends.

Assembling

Position squares (with right sides facing up) as shown in **Fig 2.** To join, hold two squares side by side. Loosely, whipstitch squares tog, working through both lps of each corresponding st across side. Join rem squares in same manner. Be sure to have each four-corner junction securely joined.

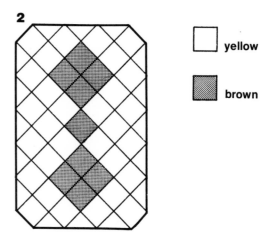

2

☐ yellow

▨ brown

Edging

With right side facing, use crochet hook and join brown with a sl st in any st around edge of afghan. **Rnd 1:** Ch 1, work in sc evenly spaced around, join with a sl st in beg sc. **Rnd 2:** Ch 1, turn; sc in each sc around, join with a sl st in beg sc. **Rnd 3:** Rep Rnd 2. Finish off; weave in all ends. Lightly steam press joinings on wrong side.

knitted panels
DESERT FLOWER

designed by Jean Leinhauser

SIZE: Approx 48″ x 66″

MATERIALS
Worsted weight yarn: 20 oz light salmon;
20 oz dark salmon
Size 13, 14″ straight knitting needles (or size required for gauge)
Size J aluminum crochet hook (for edging only)

GAUGE: In patt st, 8 sts = 2″

INSTRUCTIONS
Center Panel
With lt salmon, CO 96 sts *loosely*. Work in pattern stitch as follows.

Row 1 (wrong side): Wrapping yarn twice around needle for each st, purl across.

Row 2: * Sl 4 sts to right-hand needle, dropping extra wraps; sl these 4 elongated sts back onto left-hand needle; then (K4 tog, P4 tog) twice into these same 4 sts; rep from * across.

Row 3: P2; wrapping yarn twice around needle for each st, purl across to last 2 sts; P2.

Row 4: K2; rep from * of Row 2 to last 2 sts, K2.

Rep Rows 1 through 4 until work measures approx 66″ long, ending by working Row 2 or Row 4. BO all sts *loosely* in purl. Do not finish off; work edging around panel as follows.

Edging: Insert crochet hook in last lp of bind-off. With right side facing, work one rnd in sc evenly spaced (approx one st in each row across long edges and one st in every other st across short edges) around panel, working 3 sc in each corner. Be sure to have the same number of sts along each side edge for sewing panels tog later. Join with a sl st in beg sc; finish off. Weave in ends.

Side Panel (make 2)
With dk salmon, CO 48 sts *loosely*. Work same as Center Panel.

Assembling
To join, hold two panels with right sides tog. Thread dk salmon into a tapestry needle. Carefully matching sts and working in **outer lps only,** sew long edges tog, using overcast st. Join rem panel in same manner.

knitted strips
WHITBY TWEED
designed by Mary Thomas

Using 2 strands of yarn and combining colors to produce a woven effect, this pattern works up quickly on size 19 needles.

SIZE: Approx 48″ x 72″ without tassels

MATERIALS
Worsted weight yarn: 24 oz ecru;
28 oz brown
Size 19 straight knitting needles (or size required or gauge)

Materials Note: Yarn is used doubled throughout patt.

**GAUGE: With 2 strands of yarn in patt st,
5 sts = 2″; 13 rows = 4″**

PATTERN STITCH (multiple of 2 + 1)

Row 1: * K1, bring yarn to front of work, sl 1 as to purl; bring yarn to back of work; rep from * to last st, K1.

Row 2: K1, P1; * bring yarn to back of work, sl 1 as to purl; bring yarn to front of work, P1; rep from * to last st, K1.

Rep Rows 1 and 2 for patt.

INSTRUCTIONS

[**Note:** *Yarn is used doubled throughout patt.*]

Strip A (make 4)

With 2 strands of brown, CO 17 sts. Following *Pattern Stitch* instructions, work 26 rows in each of the following color combinations:

  2 strands brown
  1 strand each brown and ecru
  2 strands ecru
  1 strand each brown and ecru
  2 strands brown
  1 strand each brown and ecru
  2 strands ecru
  1 strand each brown and ecru
  2 strands brown

At end of last color combination, BO all sts. Weave in all ends.

Strip B (make 3)

With 2 strands of ecru, CO 17 sts. Following *Pattern Stitch* instructions, work 26 rows in each of the following color combinations:

  2 strands ecru
  1 strand each ecru and brown
  2 strands brown
  1 strand each ecru and brown
  2 strands ecru
  1 strand each ecru and brown
  2 strands brown
  1 strand each ecru and brown
  2 strands ecru

At end of last color combination, BO all sts. Weave in all ends.

Assembling

Arrange strips side by side, having A and B Strips alternating, and CO edge of each strip at same end of afghan. With brown, sew panels tog, carefully matching rows.

Tassel (make 16)

Cut a piece of cardboard about 6" wide, and 7" long. Wind brown yarn around length of cardboard, 40 times. Cut 20" strand of brown, and thread into tapestry needle doubled. Insert needle through all strands at top of cardboard, pull up tightly and knot securely, leaving ends for attaching to afghan. Cut yarn at opposite end of cardboard **(Fig 1)**; remove cardboard.

Cut another strand of brown, 10" long, and wrap it tightly twice around tassel 1" below top knot. Knot securely and allow excess ends to fall as part of tassel.

Attach one tassel at each edge and at each joining along each short end of afghan.

knitted strips
GOLDEN GLOW

designed by Mary Thomas

SIZE: Approx 44″ x 60″

MATERIALS
Worsted weight yarn: 20 oz light yellow; 24 oz medium gold
Size 10, 14″ straight knitting needles (or size required for gauge)
Cable needle

GAUGE: In garter st, 13 sts = 3″

INSTRUCTIONS
Strip (make 7 total: 3 yellow and 4 gold)
CO 24 sts. Knit first 4 rows.

Inc Row: K6, inc in next st [**To Inc: Knit in front and back of st = inc made.**]; K2, inc in next st; K4, inc in next st; K2, inc in next st; K6 = 28 sts. Now work in pattern stitch as follows.

Row 1 (right side): K2, RT (right twist) [**To Make RT: K2 tog but do not remove from left-hand needle (Fig 1); insert tip of right-hand needle into first st (Fig 2) and**

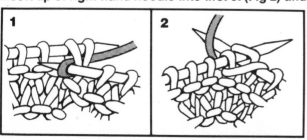

knit it again, then sl both sts off left-hand needle = **RT made.**]; (K2, P2) twice, K4; (P2, K2) twice, RT, K2.

Row 2: K2, P2, K4; P2, K2, P4; K2, P2, K4; P2, K2.

Rows 3 through 6: Rep Rows 1 and 2, twice.

Row 7 (cable twist row): K2, RT, K2; P2, sl next 4 sts onto cable needle and hold at **back** of work; knit next 2 sts, then P2, K2 from cable needle; sl next 2 sts onto cable needle and hold at **front** of work; K2, P2, then K2 from cable needle; P2, K2, RT, K2.

Row 8: Rep Row 2.

Rows 9 and 10: Rep Rows 1 and 2.

Row 11: Rep Row 1.

Row 12: K2, P2, knit to last 4 sts; P2, K2.

Row 13: K2, RT, knit to last 4 sts; RT, K2.

Rows 14 and 15: Rep Rows 12 and 13.

Row 16: Rep Row 12.

Rep Rows 1 through 16 until strip measures approx 59″ long, ending by working Row 11.

Dec Row: K6, K2 tog; K2, K2 tog; K4, K2 tog; K2, K2 tog; K6 = 24 sts. Knit 4 more rows; then BO all sts in knit.

Assembling
Arrange strips side by side, alternating colors. Be sure to have BO edge of each strip at same end of afghan. With gold, sew strips tog, carefully matching garter st ridges. Weave in all ends.

Persimmon – page 15

Rainbow Ripple – page 18

Kittens – page 20

Blue Skies – page 16

Colorado Stripes – page 14

Contemporary Granny – page 25

Burgundy Honeycomb – page 13

Lemon Lime Sherbet – page 12

Criss Cross – page 19

Granny Ripple – page 17

82

Aran Isles – page 36

Springtime Ripple – page 21

Highland Glen – page 31

Victorian Lace – page 11

Spring Flower – page 41

Empress Coverlet – page 33

Fall Leaves – page 23

Christmas Granny – page 39

Irish Mist – page 27

Autumn Glory – page 35

84

Golden Amber – page 47

Snowflowers – page 45

Log Cabin – page 63

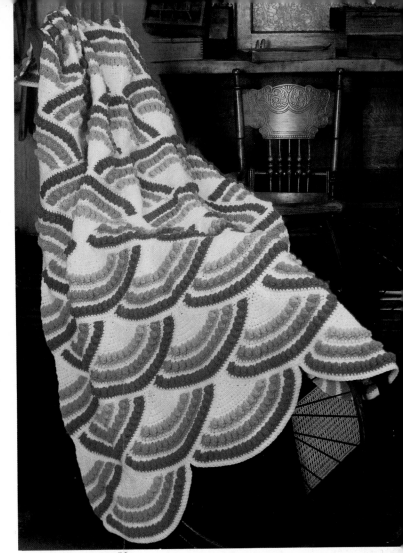

Clamshell – page 52

Moorish Tiles – page 129

Daisy Field – page 51

Diagonal Diamonds – page 56

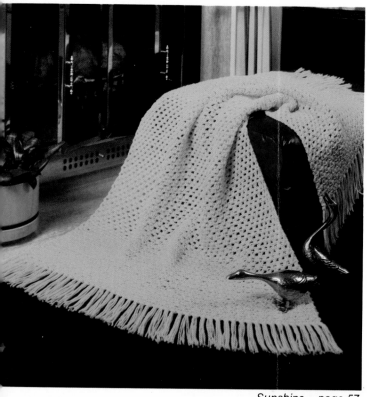

Sunshine – page 57

Afghan, Afghan – page 58

Fiesta – page 55

Desert Flower – page 77

Williamsburg – page 66　　　　*Whitby Tweed – page 78*

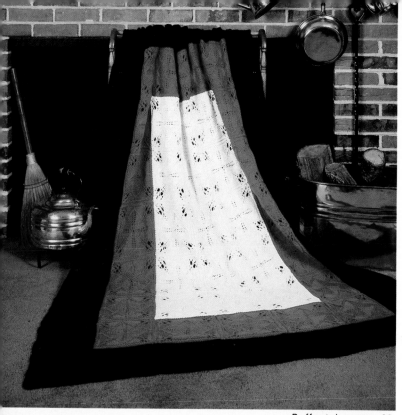

Puffpetal – page 68

Chocolate Medallion – page 74

Desert Sunset – page 100

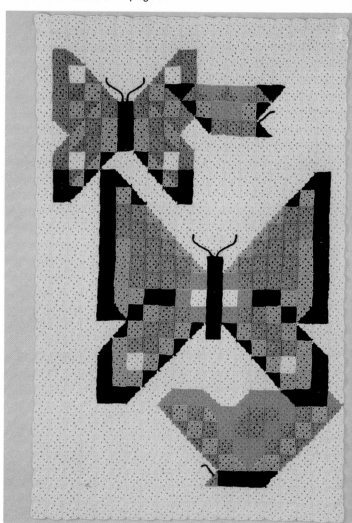

Butterflies – page 110

Six-Pointed Star – page 61

Sunrise – page 140

Springtime – page 141

Jungle Friends – page 106

Harvest Festival – page 49

English Garden – page 118

Geranium – page 72

Dutch Pinwheels – page 98

Starflower – page 70

Sweet Violets – page 130

Tulip Quilt – page 114

Imperial Garden – page 125

Indian Blanket – page 134

Victorian Roses – page 122

Bedtime Tales – page 136

Spearmint Leaves – page 133

Morning Glory – page 142

Snowbaby – page 149

Sweet Dreams – page 145

Forget-Me-Not – page 143

Happy Event – page 147

Baby Rickrack – page 144

Golden Glow – page 80

Raspberry Flip – page 154

Two-Tone Lace — page 153

Ruffles and Lace — page 156

Candy Mint — page 152

Light and Lovely — page 158

Peek-a-Boo — page 159

Magic Castle – page 108   *Ship of Dreams – page 112*

Party Time – page 102   *Grandpa's Farm – page 104*

Chapter 6

Picture Afghans

These delightful afghans are fascinating to make, and are spectacular gifts. The pictorial and geometric designs are created from 2¼ " granny squares, some worked in two colors. Details are added with chains or other shapes, which are appliquéd to the finished afghan.

Two of the designs, *Ship of Dreams* and *Tulip Quilt,* are adapted from antique quilts owned by Mary Thomas.

We suggest that you work from the top to the bottom of the afghans, sewing the squares together every two or three rows. This makes it more exciting as the picture develops gradually.

Once you've started making picture afghans, you'll find they're a bit like popcorn—you just can't stop!

GENERAL INSTRUCTIONS

Basic Granny Square Patterns

One-Color Square
Ch 4, join with a sl st to form a ring.

Rnd 1 (wrong side): Ch 3, 2 dc in ring **(Fig 1);** ch 2, (3 dc in ring, ch 2) 3 times; join with a sl st in top of beg ch-3 **(Fig 2).**

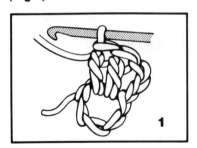

Rnd 2: Turn; sk joining st, sl st in next ch st and into ch-2 sp; ch 3, 2 dc in same sp; * ch 1, work (3 dc, ch 2, 3 dc) all in next ch-2 sp for corner; rep from * twice more; ch 1, 3 dc in beg corner sp **(Fig 3)**; ch 2, join with a sl st in top of beg ch-3. Finish off, leaving 8″ sewing length for joining later.

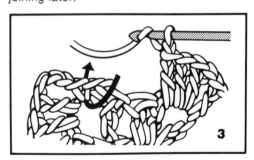

Two-Color Square
With center color, ch 4, join with a sl st to form a ring.

Rnd 1 (wrong side): Ch 3, 2 dc in ring; (ch 2, 3 dc in ring) 3 times, ch 2; join with a sl st in top of beg ch-3. Finish off center color.

Rnd 2: Turn; join second color with a sl st in any ch-2 sp; ch 3, 2 dc in same sp; * ch 1, work (3 dc, ch 2, 3 dc) all in next ch-2 sp for corner; rep from * twice more; ch 1, 3 dc in beg corner sp; ch 2, join with a sl st in top of beg ch-3. Finish off, leaving approx 8″ sewing length.

Diagonal Two-Color Squares

[**Notes:** Individual patterns list two colors for Diagonal Squares. When making squares, use either color for "color A" and the other color for "color B." When joining squares later, be sure to match colors of adjacent squares to form pictures.]

With color A, ch 4, join with a sl st to form a ring.

Rnd 1 (wrong side): Ch 3, 2 dc in ring; ch 2, 3 dc in ring; drop color A (do not cut); with color B, ch 2 **(Fig 4)**; continuing with color B, (3 dc in ring, ch 2) twice; join with a sl st in top of beg ch-3 of color A.

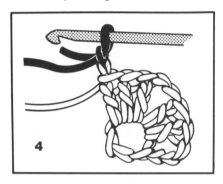

Rnd 2: Turn; sk joining st, sl st in next ch st and into ch-2 sp; ch 3, 2 dc in same sp; ch 1, work (3 dc, ch 2, 3 dc) all in next ch-2 sp for corner; ch 1, 3 dc in next ch-2 sp; ch 2, drop color B; with color A, work 3 dc in same sp, ch 1; continuing with color A, work (3 dc, ch 2, 3 dc) all in next ch-2 sp, ch 1; work 3 dc in beg corner sp (over 2 sl sts of

color B), ch 2; join with a sl st in top of beg ch-3 of color B. Finish off, leaving approx 8" sewing lengths.

Joining Squares

A chart is given with each individual pattern which shows the order in which the squares are to be joined in order to form the "picture." To join, hold two squares with right sides tog, positioned (whenever possible) so sewing length is in upper right-hand corner. Thread yarn (use matching yarn when a sewing length is not available) into tapestry needle. Carefully matching sts on both squares, sew with overcast st in outer lps only **(Fig 5)** across side, beg and ending with one corner st. You may join squares in rows across and then sew rows tog; or you may wish to sew squares forming parts of the picture, then sew these units tog. Be sure that all four-corner junctions are firmly joined.

When all squares have been joined, weave in all ends. Then steam press lightly on wrong side, if needed.

crocheted
DUTCH PINWHEELS
designed by Anis Duncan

SIZE: Approx 48" × 67"

MATERIALS
Worsted weight yarn in 4-oz skeins:
   8 skeins red;
   10 skeins turquoise;
   1 skein each bright yellow, white and dark blue
Size G aluminum crochet hook (or size required for gauge)
Materials Note: Approx 40 squares can be made from one skein of yarn.

GAUGE: One square = 2¼"

INSTRUCTIONS

Following General Instructions on page 97, make and join the required number of One-Color and Diagonal Two-Color Squares as listed for the Dutch Pinwheels Chart.

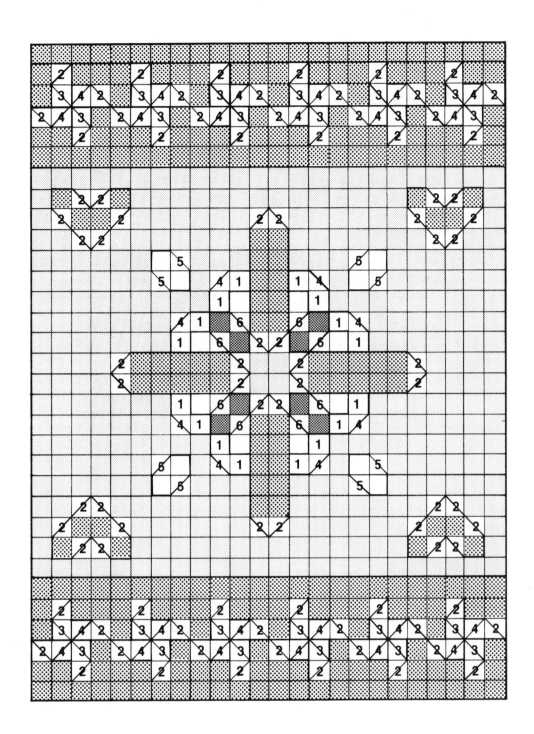

Dutch Pinwheels Chart

ONE-COLOR SQUARES

SYMBOL	COLOR	NUMBER REQUIRED
	WHITE	16
	TURQUOISE	320
	RED	248
	BLUE	8
1	YELLOW	16

DIAGONAL TWO-COLOR SQUARES

SYMBOL	COLORS	NUMBER REQUIRED
2	TURQUOISE/RED	88
3	TURQUOISE/BLUE	24
4	TURQUOISE/YELLOW	32
5	TURQUOISE/WHITE	8
6	BLUE/WHITE	8

crocheted
DESERT SUNSET
designed by Anis Duncan

SIZE: Approx 48″ × 67″

MATERIALS
Worsted weight yarn in 4-oz skeins:
   9 skeins beige;
   4 skeins blue;
   3 skeins dark green;
   2 skeins each lime green, camel and brown;
   1 skein each gold, orange and white
Size G aluminum crochet hook (or size required for gauge)
Materials Note: Approx 40 squares can be made from one skein of yarn.

GAUGE: One square = 2¼″

INSTRUCTIONS

Following General Instructions on page 97, make and join the required number of One-Color and Diagonal Two-Color Squares as listed for the Desert Sunset Chart.

Desert Sunset Chart

ONE-COLOR SQUARES

COLOR		NUMBER REQUIRED
☐	WHITE	2
▨	BLUE	122
▨	BEIGE	332
▨	DARK GREEN	84
1	BROWN	43
2	LIME GREEN	46
3	CAMEL	46
4	GOLD	19
5	ORANGE	5

DIAGONAL TWO-COLOR SQUARES

COLORS		NUMBER REQUIRED
6	BEIGE/BROWN	14
7	BLUE/WHITE	6
8	BLUE/ORANGE	2
9	BLUE/CAMEL	7
10	BLUE/BROWN	2
11	GOLD/CAMEL	5
12	GOLD/BEIGE	1
13	BROWN/CAMEL	4
14	BROWN/ORANGE	2
15	CAMEL/WHITE	2
16	CAMEL/ORANGE	2
17	LIME GREEN/ORANGE	5
18	LIME GREEN/BEIGE	11
19	LIME GREEN/BROWN	3
20	DARK GREEN/BEIGE	3

crocheted
PARTY TIME

designed by Anis Duncan

SIZE: Approx 32″ × 41″

MATERIALS
Worsted weight yarn in 4-oz skeins:
   4 skeins white;
   2 skeins brown;
   1 skein each red, blue and yellow;
   9 yards orange
**Size G aluminum crochet hook (or size required
   for gauge**
Materials Note: Approx 40 squares can be made
from one skein of yarn.

GAUGE: One square = 2¼″

INSTRUCTIONS

Following General Instructions on page 97, make and
join the required number of One-Color and Diagonal
Two-Color Squares as listed for the Party Time Chart.

When all squares have been joined, make the
following appliqué details and sew in place as shown
in photo, using matching sewing thread.

Bird's Beak: With orange, ch 2. **Row 1:** Sc in 2nd ch
from hook. **Row 2:** Ch 1, turn; 2 sc in sc. **Row 3:** Ch 1,
turn; 2 sc in each sc across = 4 sc. **Row 4:** Ch 1, turn; 2
sc in first sc, sc in each of next 2 sc, 2 sc in last sc = 6
sc. Finish off; weave in yarn ends.

Bird's Legs: With orange, make 2 chains—one 3½″
long and the other 1½″ long. Finish off; weave in yarn
ends.

Bird's Eye: With 2 strands of brown, ch 3, join with a sl
st to form a ring. Finish off; weave in yarn ends.

Bear's Ear: With orange, ch 3, join with a sl st to form a
ring. **Row 1:** Work 6 sc in ring. **Row 2:** Ch 1, turn; 2 sc in
first sc, sc in each of next 4 sc, 2 sc in last sc = 8 sc.
Row 3: Ch 1, turn; 2 sc in first sc, sc in each of next 2 sc,
2 sc in each of next 2 sc, sc in each of next 2 sc, 2 sc in
last sc = 12 sc. Finish off orange. **Row 4:** Turn; join

brown with a sl st in first sc, ch 1; 2 sc in same sc as joining, sc in each of next 2 sc; 2 sc in next sc, sc in each of
next 4 sc; 2 sc in next sc, sc in each of next 2 sc; 2 sc in
last sc = 16 sc. **Row 5:** Ch 1, turn; 2 sc in first sc, * sc in
each of next 4 sc, 2 sc in next sc; rep from * twice more
= 20 sc. **Row 6:** Ch 1, turn; sc in each sc across. Finish
off; weave in yarn ends.

Bear's Nose and Mouth: With orange, make a chain
6½″ long. Finish off; weave in yarn ends.

Bear's Eyes (make 2): With orange, ch 8, join with a sl
st to form a ring. Work (2 sc, 5 hdc, 2 sc) in ring. Finish
off; weave in yarn ends.

Bear's Belly Button: With orange, ch 4, join with a sl st
to form a ring. Work 8 sc in ring; join with a sl st in first
sc. Finish off; weave in yarn ends.

Balloon Strings: Make 2 chains as follows: with blue,
make one chain 13″ long; then with red, make another
chain 20½″ long. Finish off; weave in yarn ends.

Party Hat Pompon: With red, make a 1″ diameter pompon as follows. Cut two cardboard circles, each 1½″ in
diameter. Cut a hole in the center of each circle approx
½″ in diameter. Thread a tapestry needle with a 72″
length of yarn doubled. Holding both circles tog, insert
needle through center hole, over outside edge, through
center again **(Fig 1)**, until entire circle is covered (thread
more lengths of yarn as needed). With scissors, cut yarn
between the two circles all around the circumference
(Fig 2). Using a 12″ strand of yarn doubled, slip yarn between circles, pull up tightly and tie very firmly. Remove
cardboards, and fluff out pompon by rolling it between
your hands. Trim evenly with scissors.

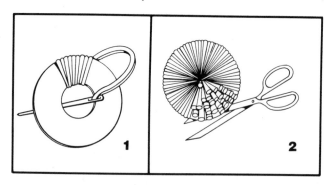

Party Time Chart

ONE-COLOR SQUARES

SYMBOL	COLOR	NUMBER REQUIRED
	WHITE	139
	YELLOW	26
	RED	33
	BROWN	45
1	BLUE	24

DIAGONAL TWO-COLOR SQUARES

COLORS		NUMBER REQUIRED
2	YELLOW/WHITE	5
3	YELLOW/BROWN	1
4	BLUE/WHITE	4
5	RED/WHITE	4
6	BROWN/WHITE	19

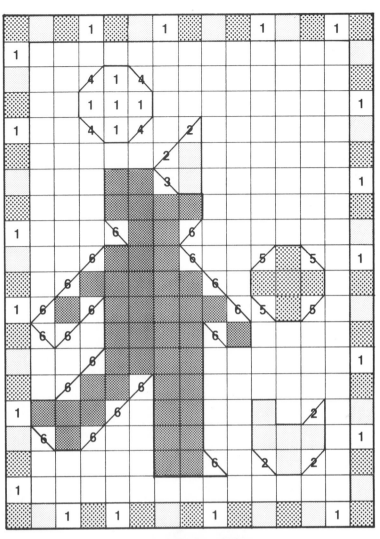

103

crocheted
GRANDPA'S FARM

designed by Anis Duncan

SIZE: Approx 45″ × 68″

MATERIALS

American Thread Dawn Sayelle* Worsted Size Yarn in 4-oz skeins:
- 4 skeins Premier Green;
- 3 skeins each Grass Green and True Blue;
- 2 skeins each Forest Green and White;
- 1 skein each Coffee, Black and Flame Red

Size G aluminum crochet hook (or size required for gauge)

Materials Note: Approx 40 squares can be made from one skein of yarn.

GAUGE: One square = 2¼″

INSTRUCTIONS

Following General Instructions on page 97, make and join the required number of One-Color, Two-Color and Diagonal Two-Color Squares as listed for the Grandpa's Farm Chart.

When all squares have been joined, make the following appliqué detail and sew in place as shown in photo, using matching sewing thread.

Roof (for house in upper left corner): With 2 strands of Black, make a chain approx 7″ long. Finish off; weave in yarn ends.

Grandpa's Farm Chart

ONE-COLOR SQUARES

SYMBOL	COLOR	NUMBER REQUIRED
1	COFFEE	35
2	FOREST GREEN	35
3	BLACK	23
4	FLAME RED	24
■	GRASS GREEN	88
▨	PREMIER GREEN	154
▨	TRUE BLUE	83
□	WHITE	63

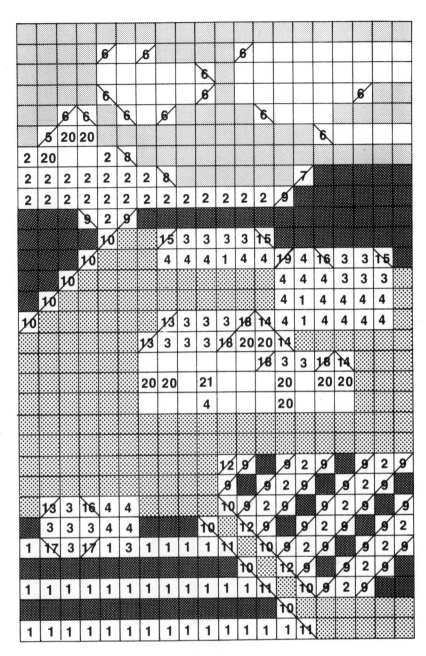

DIAGONAL TWO-COLOR SQUARES

	COLORS	NUMBER REQUIRED
5	BLACK/TRUE BLUE	1
6	TRUE BLUE/WHITE	13
7	TRUE BLUE/GRASS GREEN	1
8	TRUE BLUE/FOREST GREEN	2
9	GRASS GREEN/FOREST GREEN	31
10	PREMIER GREEN/GRASS GREEN	11
11	PREMIER GREEN/COFFEE	3
12	PREMIER GREEN/FOREST GREEN	3
13	PREMIER GREEN/BLACK	3
14	PREMIER GREEN/WHITE	3
15	GRASS GREEN/BLACK	3
16	BLACK/FLAME RED	2
17	BLACK/COFFEE	2
18	BLACK/WHITE	4
19	GRASS GREEN/FLAME RED	1

TWO-COLOR SQUARES

SYMBOL	COLORS	NUMBER REQUIRED
20	BLACK (CENTER)/WHITE	11
21	BLACK (CENTER)/FLAME RED	1

crocheted
JUNGLE FRIENDS

designed by Anis Duncan

SIZE: Approx 45" × 68"

MATERIALS
American Thread Dawn Sayelle* Worsted Size
Yarn in 4-oz skeins:
   4 skeins Turquoise;
   3 skeins each Grass Green, Premier Green and
      Steel Gray;
   2 skeins each Antique Gold and Coffee;
   1 skein each Wood Brown and White
   1½ yards Black
Size G aluminum crochet hook (or size required
   for gauge)
Materials Note: Approx 40 squares can be made
from one skein of yarn.

GAUGE: One square = 2¼"

INSTRUCTIONS

Following General Instructions on page 97, make and join the required number of One-Color and Diagonal Two-Color Squares as listed for the Jungle Friends Chart.

When all squares have been joined, make the following applique details and sew in place as shown in photo, using matching sewing thread.

Camel's Facial Features: With Wood Brown, make 3 chains—make first chain 9" long for nose and mouth; make next chain 4" long for ear; and make last chain 2½" long for eye. Finish off; weave in yarn ends. **Note:** Sew to afghan with back ridge of chain facing you.

Elephant's Eye: With Black, make a chain 7" long. Finish off; weave in yarn ends. **Note:** Sew to afghan with back ridge of chain facing you.

Elephant's Ear (outline): With 2 strands of Steel Gray, make a chain 18" long. Finish off; weave in yarn ends. **Note:** Sew to afghan with back ridge of chain facing you.

Elephant's Tusk: With White, ch 7. **Row 1:** Sc in 2nd ch from hook and in each rem ch across = 6 sc. **Row 2:** Ch 1, turn; sc in each sc across. **Rows 3 and 4:** Rep Row 2, twice. **Row 5:** Ch 1, turn; 2 sc in first sc, sc in each of next 3 sc; dec over last 2 sc **[To Work Dec: Draw up a lp in each of next 2 sc, YO and draw through all 3 lps on hook = dec made.]** = 6 sc. **Row 6:** Rep Row 2. **Row 7:** Rep Row 5. **Rows 8 through 17:** Rep Row 2, ten times. **Row 18:** Rep Row 5. **Row 19:** Rep Row 2. **Row 20:** Rep Row 5. **Row 21:** Rep Row 2. **Row 22:** Rep Row 5. **Row 23:** Ch 1, turn; dec over first 2 sts, sc in each rem sc across = 5 sc. **Row 24:** Ch 1, turn; 2 sc in first sc, sc in each of next 2 sc, dec over last 2 sts = 5 sc. **Row 25:** Ch 1, turn; (dec over 2 sts) twice, 2 sc in last st = 4 sc. **Row 26:** Ch 1, turn; 2 sc in first sc, sc in next sc, dec over last 2 sts = 4 sc. **Row 27:** Ch 1, turn; dec over first 2 sts, sc in each of last 2 sc = 3 sc. **Row 28:** Ch 1, turn; sc in first sc, dec over last 2 sts = 2 sc. **Row 29:** Ch 1, turn; dec over 2 sts. Finish off; weave in yarn ends.

Jungle Friends Chart

ONE-COLOR SQUARES

SYMBOL	COLOR	NUMBER REQUIRED
1	COFFEE	51
2	ANTIQUE GOLD	49
3	WOOD BROWN	22
▓	GRASS GREEN	71
░	PREMIER GREEN	88
▒	STEEL GRAY	90
☐	TURQUOISE	162

DIAGONAL TWO-COLOR SQUARES

	COLORS	NUMBER REQUIRED
4	TURQUOISE/GRASS GREEN	39
5	TURQUOISE/STEEL GRAY	5
6	TURQUOISE/ANTIQUE GOLD	2
7	TURQUOISE/WOOD BROWN	1
8	STEEL GRAY/COFFEE	1
9	STEEL GRAY/WOOD BROWN	2
10	ANTIQUE GOLD/STEEL GRAY	6
11	WOOD BROWN/COFFEE	1
12	PREMIER GREEN/WOOD BROWN	4
13	ANTIQUE GOLD/COFFEE	1
14	GRASS GREEN/PREMIER GREEN	5

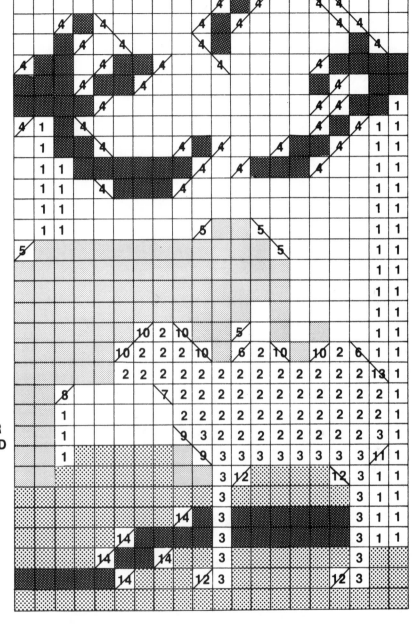

crocheted
MAGIC CASTLE

designed by Grif Stenger

SIZE: Approx 45" × 68"

MATERIALS
American Thread Dawn Sayelle* Worsted Size Yarn in 4-oz skeins:
    4 skeins each Lemon and Turquoise;
    3 skeins Grass Green;
    2 skeins each Light Gold and White;
    1 skein each True Blue, Antique Gold and Coffee
Size G aluminum crochet hook (or size required for gauge)
Materials Note: Approx 40 squares can be made from one skein of yarn.

GAUGE: One square = 2¼ "

INSTRUCTIONS

Following General Instructions on page 97, make and join the required number of One-Color, Two-Color and Diagonal Two-Color Squares as listed for the Magic Castle Chart.

When all squares have been joined, make the following applique details and sew in place as shown in photo, using matching sewing thread.

Draw Bridge Chains: With 2 strands of Antique Gold, make two chains, each 21" long. Finish off; weave in yarn ends. **Note:** Sew to afghan with back ridge of chain facing you.

Magic Castle Chart

ONE-COLOR SQUARES

SYMBOL	COLOR	NUMBER REQUIRED
☐ (white)	WHITE	53
▨ (lemon)	LEMON	131
▨ (turquoise)	TURQUOISE	145
▨ (grass green)	GRASS GREEN	111
1	TRUE BLUE	28
2	COFFEE	16
3	LIGHT GOLD	62
4	ANTIQUE GOLD	16

DIAGONAL TWO-COLOR SQUARES

COLORS	NUMBER REQUIRED
5 TURQUOISE/LIGHT GOLD	1
6 LIGHT GOLD/WHITE	3
7 TRUE BLUE/COFFEE	4
8 GRASS GREEN/COFFEE	4
9 LEMON/ANTIQUE GOLD	4
10 TURQUOISE/WHITE	12

TWO-COLOR SQUARES

COLORS	NUMBER REQUIRED
11 GOLD (CENTER)/LEMON	10

crocheted
BUTTERFLIES

designed by Anis Duncan

SIZE: Approx 45″ × 68″

MATERIALS
American Thread Dawn Sayelle* Worsted Size Yarn in 4-oz skeins:
> 10 skeins Lemon;
> 2 skeins each Turquoise, Premier Green and Lilac;
> 1 skein each Orange, Royal Blue and Black

Size G aluminum crochet hook (or size required for gauge)

Materials Note: Approx 40 squares can be made from one skein of yarn.

GAUGE: One square = 2¼″

INSTRUCTIONS

Following General Instructions on page 97, make and join the required number of One-Color and Diagonal Two-Color Squares as listed for the Butterflies Chart.

When all squares have been joined, make the following applique details and sew in place as shown in photo, using matching sewing thread.

Antennae: With Black, make two chains, each 6″ long, for center butterfly; then make one more chain 3″ long for butterfly at upper right. For rem 2 butterflies, use Royal Blue and make two chains, each 5″ long, for butterfly at upper left; then make one more chain 3″ long for butterfly at bottom edge. Finish off; weave in yarn ends.

Butterflies Chart

ONE-COLOR SQUARES

SYMBOL	COLOR	NUMBER REQUIRED
☐	LEMON	331
▨	TURQUOISE	48
▨	PREMIER GREEN	38
■	BLACK	29
1	ORANGE	18
2	LILAC	31
3	ROYAL BLUE	16

DIAGONAL TWO-COLOR SQUARES

	COLORS	NUMBER REQUIRED
4	BLACK/PREMIER GREEN	3
5	BLACK/LILAC	1
6	BLACK/LEMON	9
7	TURQUOISE/LEMON	8
8	ORANGE/LEMON	4
9	PREMIER GREEN/LEMON	18
10	LILAC/LEMON	1
11	ROYAL BLUE/LEMON	19
12	BLACK/ORANGE	1
13	PREMIER GREEN/TURQUOISE	2
14	PREMIER GREEN/LILAC	3
15	ORANGE/PREMIER GREEN	4
16	LILAC/TURQUOISE	8
17	ORANGE/LILAC	1
18	ORANGE/TURQUOISE	3
19	BLACK/TURQUOISE	2
20	BLACK/ROYAL BLUE	2

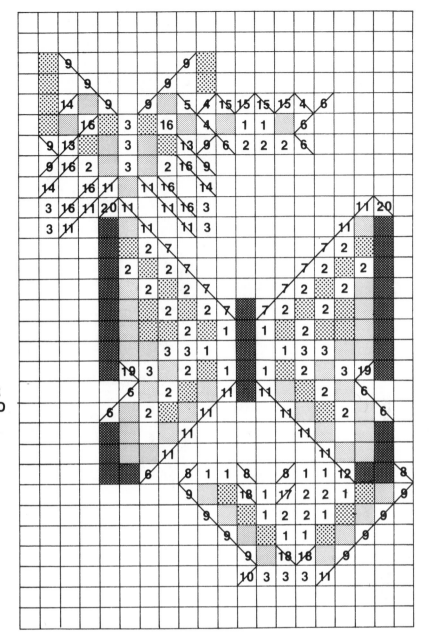

crocheted
SHIP OF DREAMS

design adapted from an antique quilt pattern

SIZE: Approx 45″ × 63″

MATERIALS
Worsted weight yarn:
   36 oz medium blue;
   18 oz white
Size G aluminum crochet hook (or size required
   for gauge)
Materials Note: Approx 40 squares can be made
from one skein of yarn.

GAUGE: One square = 2¼ ″

INSTRUCTIONS

Following General Instructions on page 97, make and
join the required number of One-Color and Diagonal
Two-Color Squares as listed for the Ship of Dreams
Chart.

Ship of Dreams Chart
ONE-COLOR SQUARES

SYMBOL	COLOR	NUMBER REQUIRED
	BLUE	288
	WHITE	112

DIAGONAL TWO-COLOR SQUARES

SYMBOL	COLORS	NUMBER REQUIRED
	BLUE/WHITE	160

crocheted
TULIP QUILT

design adapted from an antique quilt pattern

SIZE: Approx 50″ × 59″

MATERIALS
Worsted weight yarn:
   30 oz ecru;
   20 oz pink;
   7 oz dusty green;
   4 oz light orchid
**Size G aluminum crochet hook (or size required
   for gauge)**
Materials Note: Approx 40 squares can be made
from one skein of yarn.

GAUGE: One square = 2¼″

INSTRUCTIONS

Following General Instructions on page 97, make and
join the required number of One-Color and Diagonal
Two-Color Squares as listed for the Tulip Quilt Chart.

When all squares have been joined, make the following
applique details and sew in place as shown in photo, using matching sewing thread; then work edging.

Flower Stems (make 6): With green, ch 3. **Row 1:** Sc in
2nd ch from hook and in next ch = 2 sc. **Row 2:** Ch 1,
turn; sc in each sc across. Rep Row 2 until stem measures 11¼″ long. Finish off; weave in yarn ends.

Edging: With right side facing, join pink with a sl st in
right-hand corner sp of any square, ch 1. Work as follows across each square around afghan: sc in corner sp
and in each of next 3 dc; (sc, ch 3, sc) in ch-1 sp (between pair of 3-dc groups); sc in each of next 3 dc and in
corner sp. In each corner sp of afghan, work (sc, ch 3,
sc). Join with a sl st in beg sc. Finish off; weave in yarn
ends.

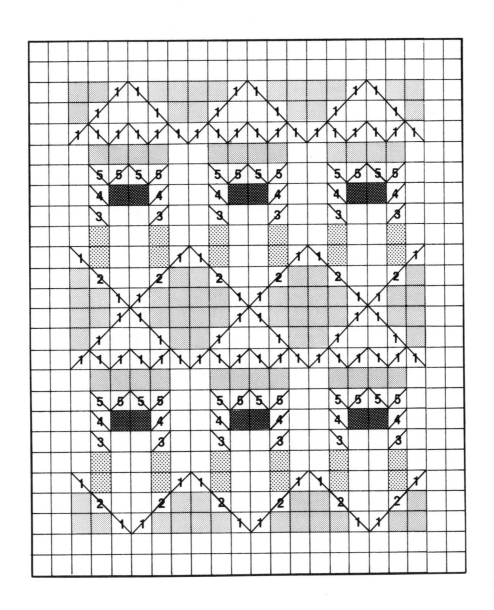

Tulip Quilt Chart

ONE-COLOR SQUARES

SYMBOL	COLOR	NUMBER REQUIRED
	ECRU	296
	PINK	96
	GREEN	24
	ORCHID	12

DIAGONAL TWO-COLOR SQUARES

SYMBOL	COLORS	NUMBER REQUIRED
1	PINK/WHITE	84
2	PINK/GREEN	12
3	GREEN/WHITE	12
4	ORCHID/WHITE	12
5	PINK/ORCHID	24

Chapter 7

The Versatile Afghan Stitch

BASIC AFGHAN STITCH

Afghan stitch begins with a foundation chain, as in regular crochet. Instead of each stitch being completed as a single unit, afghan stitch requires a two-step technique of working forward and then backward over the entire width of the work in order to complete the stitches of a row. The first step is worked forward from *right* to *left* drawing up loops (called bars) all of which are left on the hook; then without turning the work, the second step is worked backward from *left* to *right* locking each bar (loop) into an upright position.

Ch loosely the number specified in patt instructions (for practice, ch 20).

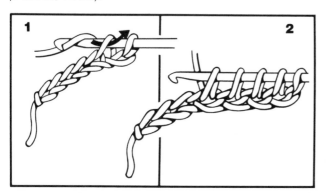

Row 1 (foundation row): Step One: Retaining lp already on hook, draw up a lp through **top lp only** of 2nd ch from hook and retain on hook **(Fig 1)**; * draw up a lp through **top lp only** of next ch and retain on hook; rep from * across **(Fig 2)**. There should now be the same number of lps (bars) on hook as number of starting chs.

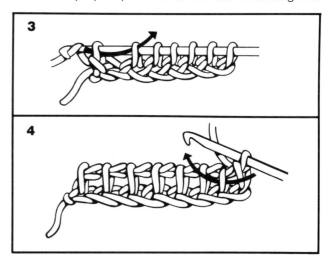

Step Two: *Do not turn;* YO hook and draw through first lp on hook; * YO hook and draw through 2 lps on hook **(Fig 3);** rep from * across. One lp now remains on hook; this is the first lp (bar) of next row.

Row 2 (patt row): Step One: With first lp already on hook, draw up a lp under 2nd bar **(Fig 4)** and retain on hook; * draw up a lp under next bar and retain on hook;

rep from * across to last bar; draw up a lp under last bar **(Fig 5)** and retain on hook. Now count lps; there should still be the same number of lps as number of starting chs.

Step Two: Same as Step Two in Row 1.

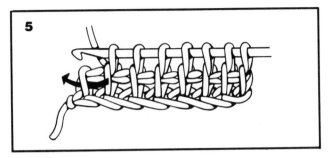

Rep Row 2 (both steps) for Basic Afghan Stitch. Your work will begin to look like **Fig 6.** [**Note:** *Remember that each row should have the same number of bars (lps) as number of starting chs.*]

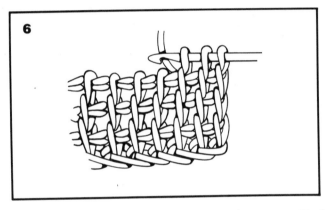

When you have completed the number of rows specified in patt, you will need to bind off which finishes the last row by firming the top edge and eliminating holes.

Bind Off: Sl st across last row as follows: * insert hook under next bar, YO hook and draw lp *loosely* through bar and lp on hook - **Fig 7;** rep from * across. Unless otherwise specified, finish off by cutting yarn and drawing through last lp on hook.

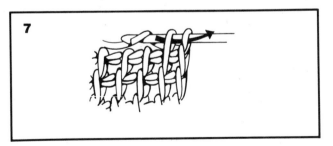

EDGING ON AFGHAN STITCH

Upon completion of your piece in afghan stitch (square, block, strip, panel, afghan), an edging may be worked either in rows along one or more edges or in rnds around the entire piece. To have neat and even edges, *it is important to work the first row/rnd correctly.* Look at diagram in **Fig 8** for placement of stitches. *Across bottom edge* along foundation chain, each st is worked under both unused lps of ch. *Across top edge* along bound-off edge of last row, each st is worked under both loops of sl st. *Across each side edge* along end of rows, each st is worked in sp at bottom of end st.

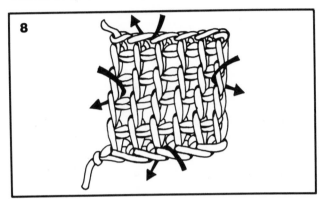

[**Note:** *Always work each st under more than one strand of yarn.*] Edging should lie flat without puckering; if necessary, do not hesitate to change hook size.

CROSS STITCH ON AFGHAN STITCH

Cross stitch on afghan stitch is worked from a chart with a key to the colors used. Each square on chart represents one bar. One cross stitch is worked over one vertical bar. [**Note:** *If an edging has been worked along each side edge of afghan, there will be 2 less bars in each row for cross stitches.*]

To work cross stitch, thread tapestry needle with desired length of yarn. Count over required number of bars to where you wish to begin. Bring yarn through from back of work to front, leaving 1″ end to be worked over (do not knot). Work cross stitches as shown in **Fig 9,** being careful not to pull stitches too tightly. Be sure that the top cross of each stitch lies in the same direction. Do not make knots; weave in all ends through sts on back of afghan.

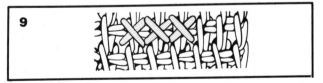

afghan stitch
with cross stitch design

ENGLISH GARDEN

designed by Jane Cannon Meyers
and Carol Wilson Mansfield

This lovely afghan is made in sections, using afghan stitch. The sections are then embroidered and joined. A scalloped edging adds the final touch.

SIZE: Approx 54″ x 70″

MATERIALS
Worsted weight yarn (for afghan):
   16 oz light teal blue;
   28 oz dark teal blue;
   12 oz white

Persian type crewel yarn (3 ply) for embroidery:
   6 yds pale yellow; 34 yds bright yellow;
   12 yds each bright orange and tangerine;
   16 yds brick;
   24 yds pink; 40 yds coral;
   28 yds light plum; 36 yds dark plum;
   18 yds purple;
   48 yds olive green; 76 yds forest green;
   8 yds brown
Size J afghan hook (or size required for gauge)
Size G aluminum crochet hook (for joining and edging)

Size 18 tapestry needle (for embroidery)

GAUGE: In afghan st, 4 sts = 1″; 3 rows = 1″

INSTRUCTIONS

MOTIF A
(solid color)
(make 13)
With afghan hook and dk blue, ch 41 *loosely*. Following *Basic Afghan Stitch* instructions on page 116, work 41 rows even in afghan st. At end of last row, bind off (see instructions on page 117). [**Note:** Mark this edge for top of motif.]

MOTIF B
(floral design)
(make 12)
With afghan hook and lt blue, ch 41 *loosely*.
Rows 1 and 2: Work 2 rows even in afghan st.
Row 3: Step One: With first lp already on hook, draw up 19 more lps; drop lt blue (do not cut); pick up white from behind work (leave approx 4″ end for weaving in later) and draw up one more lp; drop white (do not cut); with new ball of lt blue (pick up from behind work), draw up 20 more lps = 41 lps. **Step Two:** Continuing with lt blue, YO and draw through first lp on hook; (YO and draw through 2 lps on hook) 19 times; drop lt blue (do not cut); with white (pick up white from underneath — twists the two colors

118

and prevents a hole in your work as shown in **Fig 1**), YO and draw through 2 lps on hook (one lp each of lt blue and white); drop white (do not cut); with next lt blue (pick up color from underneath), * YO and draw through 2 lps on hook; rep from * across.

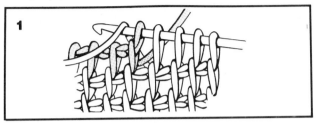

Now compare your work to the chart in **Fig 2.** You have just completed the first 3 rows. Continuing in afghan st and changing colors as indicated (in same manner as prev row), work the next 38 rows from the chart (beg with Row 4 and work through Row 41). Each square on chart represents one bar (lp). Each row on chart is worked from right to left (remember that it requires 2 steps to complete one row in afghan st). At end of last row, bind off. [**Note:** Mark this edge for top of motif.]

Fig 2

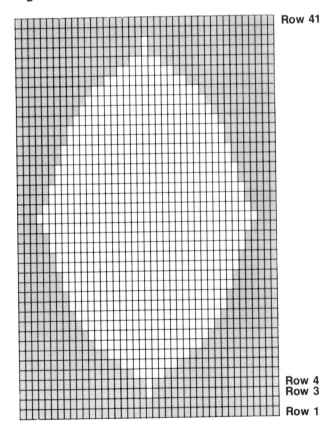

Row 41

Row 4
Row 3

Row 1

Embroidery

First read instructions for *Cross Stitch on Afghan Stitch* on page 117. Each motif has 41 sts (bars) across and 41 rows from bottom to top edge. Using full strand of Persian-type yarn, embroider 3 motifs of each floral design: flower #1 (chart in **Fig 3**), flower #2 (chart in **Fig 4**), flower #3 (chart in **Fig 5**), and flower #4 (chart in **Fig 6**). [**Note:** Remember to keep marked edge of motif at top.]

Assembling

Arrange motifs as shown in **Fig 7,** having right sides facing up and marked edge of each motif facing top edge of afghan.

Fig 7

4				1
	1	2	3	
	4		4	
	3	2	1	
2				3

First, join motifs in rows. To join, place two motifs (with right sides facing up) side by side with top edge (bound-off edge) of one motif to your right and bottom edge (foundation chain edge) to your left. Holding yarn at back of work, work sl sts on right side, alternating from edge to edge, as follows. With crochet hook, join dk blue with a sl st in st at bottom edge of right motif. Insert hook in corresponding st at bottom edge of left motif; hook yarn from beneath work and draw up through work and lp on hook (sl st made). Now work sl st in next st on right motif; then work a sl st in corresponding st on left motif. Continue working in this manner (alternating sl sts from edge to edge) until motifs are joined; finish off. Now join rem 3 motifs in same manner to complete first row; then join rem motifs into rows. Continuing to join in same manner, join rows tog, carefully matching rows and joinings.

Edging

[**Note:** *All rnds are worked on right side.*] With right side facing and top edge of afghan across top, use crochet hook and join dk blue with a sl st in st at upper right-hand corner.

Rnd 1: Ch 1, (sc, ch 1, sc) in same st for corner; working in each st across top edge (do not work into joinings), * sc in each of next 3 sts, dec over next 2 sts [**To Work Dec: Draw up a lp in each of the 2 sts, YO and draw through all 3 lps on hook = dec made.**]; rep from * to within 4 sts of next corner; sc in each of next 3 sts, (sc, ch 1, sc) in last st for corner. Continuing across side edge along end of rows, sc in each row (do not work into joinings) across. Work rem two edges in same manner; join with a sl st in beg sc. You should have between ch-1 corner sps, 161 sc across each top and bottom edge, and 207 sc across each side edge.

Rnd 2: Ch 3, do not turn; * (dc, ch 1, dc) in ch-1 corner sp; dc in each dc to next corner sp; rep from * 3 times more, join with a sl st in top of beg ch-3.

Rnd 3: Ch 1, do not turn; sc in next dc, * ch 2, sc in ch-1 corner sp; ch 2, sc in next dc; work (ch 2, sk one dc, sc in next dc) across to next corner sp; rep from * 3 times more, ending ch 2, join with a sl st in beg sc.

Rnd 4: Do not turn; sl st into next ch-2 sp; ch 3, 2 dc in same sp; * ch 1, sc in next ch-2 sp; ch 1, 3 dc in next ch-2 sp; rep from * around, ending last rep by working sl st in top of beg ch-3 instead of 3 dc in next ch-2 sp. Finish off; weave in all ends. Lightly steam press on wrong side.

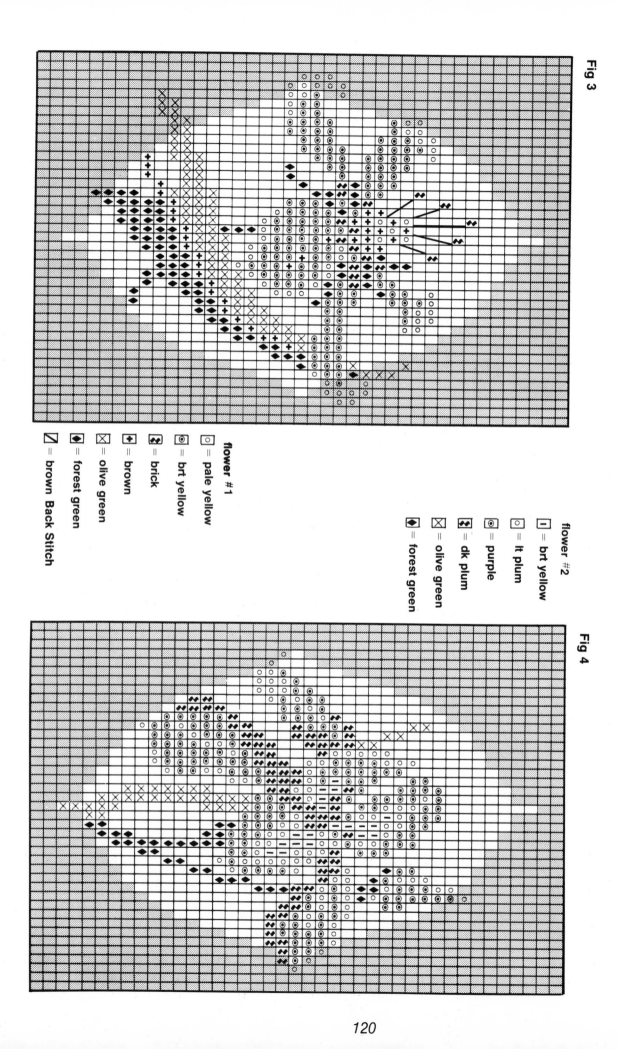

Fig 3

flower #1

⊡ = pale yellow
⊙ = brt yellow
✕ = brick
✚ = brown
✕ = olive green
◆ = brown
◆ = forest green
◢ = brown Back Stitch

flower #2

— = brt yellow
⊡ = lt plum
⊙ = purple
✕ = dk plum
✕ = olive green
◆ = forest green

Fig 4

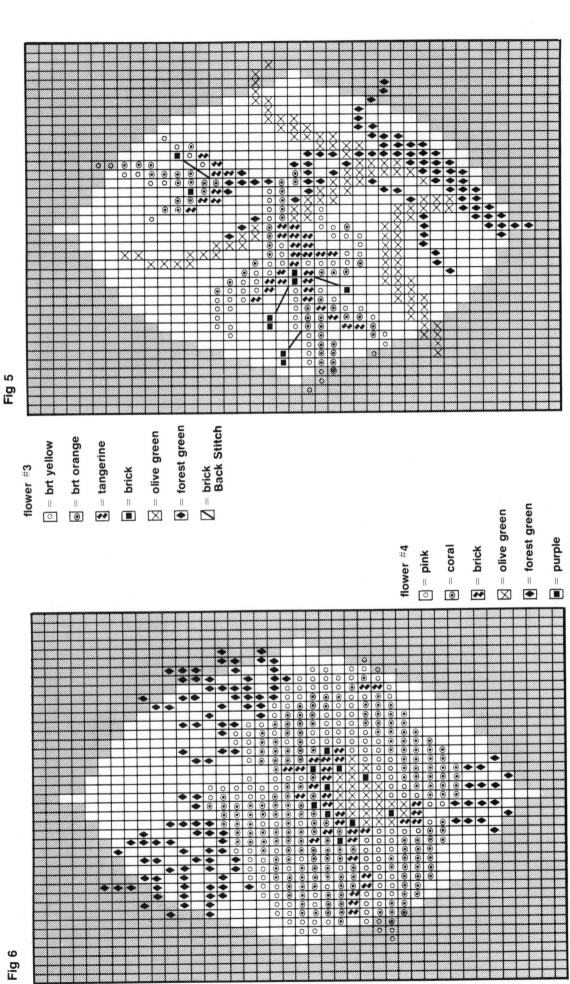

Fig 5

flower #3

○	= brt yellow
◉	= brt orange
〰	= tangerine
■	= brick
⊠	= olive green
◆	= forest green
╱	= brick Back Stitch

Fig 6

flower #4

○	= pink
◉	= coral
〰	= brick
⊠	= olive green
◆	= forest green
■	= purple

afghan stitch
with cross stitch design
VICTORIAN ROSES

SIZE: Approx 60″ x 72″ before fringing

MATERIALS
American Thread Dawn Sayelle* Worsted Size Yarn in 4-oz skeins:
For afghan:	**15 skeins Fisherman**
For embroidery:	**1 skein Candy Pink;**
	2 skeins Pink;
	2 skeins Hot Pink;
	2 skeins Nile Green

Size J afghan hook (or size required for gauge)
Size J aluminum crochet hook (for trim, joining and edging)
Size 16 tapestry needle (for embroidery)
Materials Note: Candy Pink is the lightest shade of pink, followed by Pink and Hot Pink (brightest shade).

GAUGE: In afghan st, 4 sts = 1″; 3 rows = 1″

INSTRUCTIONS

PANEL
(make 4)
With afghan hook and Fisherman, ch 56 *loosely*. Following *Basic Afghan Stitch* instruction on page 116, work 216 rows even in afghan stitch. At end of last row, bind off (see instructions on page 117).

Embroidery: First read instructions for *Cross Stitch on Afghan Stitch* on page 117. Your panel has 56 sts (bars) across and 216 rows from bottom to top edge. With full strand of worsted weight yarn, embroider chart in **Fig 1** as follows. Beg at bottom edge (along foundation chain) and embroider rose design by working chart from A to C once; from B to C once; then from B to D once. Then beg at bottom edge and embroider border pattern along each side edge for entire length of panel, having patterns 5 rows apart.

122

Fig 1

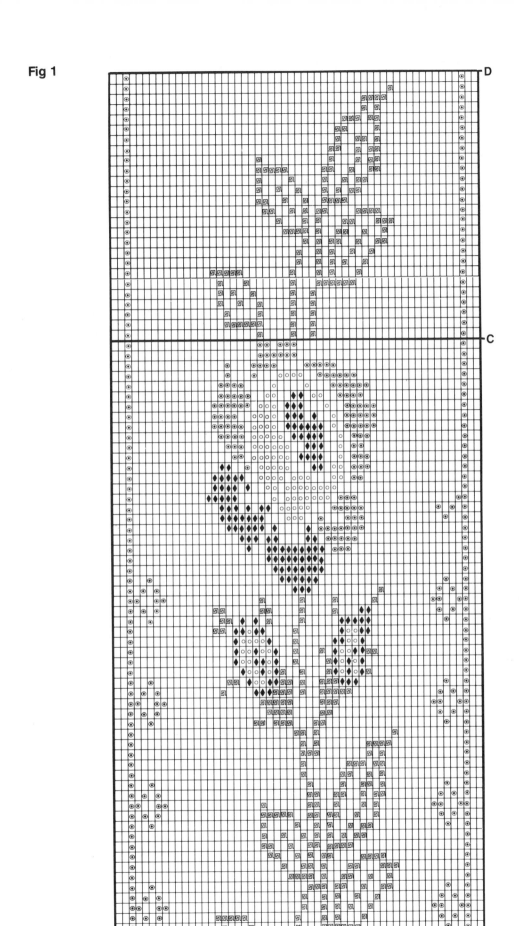

☐ = **Candy Pink**

◉ = **Pink**

◆ = **Hot Pink**

▩ = **Nile Green**

PANEL TRIM

Work trim on side edges of two center panels (for joining) as follows.

Left Trim: Hold panel with right side facing, top (bound-off) edge to your right, and side edge across top. With crochet hook, join Fisherman with a sl st in BO st at upper right-hand corner. **Row 1:** Ch 4, sk first row, dc in next row; * ch 1, sk next row, dc in next row; rep from * across, ending dc in last row at upper left-hand corner. Finish off.

Right Trim: Hold panel with right side facing, bottom (foundation chain) edge to your right, and side edge across top. With crochet hook, join Fisherman with a sl st in first row at upper right-hand corner. **Row 1:** Ch 4, * sk next row, dc in next row, ch 1; rep from * across, ending dc in first BO st at upper left-hand corner. Finish off.

Now work trim on rem two side panels (for joining) as follows. On one panel, work Right Trim only. On other panel, work Left Trim only.

Assembling

Place panels side by side, having panel edge without trim at each side edge of afghan. To join, hold two panels with right sides tog. Carefully matching sts of trim, use crochet hook and Fisherman and work one sc in each dc and in each ch-1 sp across. [**Note:** *Beg 3 chs of ch-4 count as one dc.*]. Join rem two panels in same manner. Weave in all ends. Lightly steam press on wrong side.

Edging

With right side facing, use crochet hook and Fisherman and work one rnd in sc evenly spaced (working 3 sc in each outer corner) around afghan. Finish off.

Fringe

Following *Fringe* instructions on page 9, make single knot fringe. Cut 16" strands of Fisherman; use 8 strands for each knot of fringe. Tie knots evenly spaced across each short end of afghan.

afghan stitch
with cross stitched design
IMPERIAL GARDEN

designed by Jane Cannon Meyers

This magnificent afghan — adapted from a traditional Oriental design — is embroidered with two shades of one color. For an alternate color choice for this cross-stitched design, we suggest using light and dark moss green.

SIZE: Approx 46″ x 64″ before fringing

MATERIALS
Worsted weight yarn:
   For afghan: **46 oz ecru**
   For embroidery: **8 oz each light and dark taupe**
Size J afghan hook with flexible extension (or size required for gauge)
Size 16 tapestry needle (for embroidery)

GAUGE: In afghan st, 4 sts = 1″; 3 rows = 1″

INSTRUCTIONS

With ecru, ch 185 *loosely*. Following *Basic Afghan Stitch* instructions on page 116, work 193 rows even in afghan stitch. At end of last row, bind off (see instructions on page 117).

Embroidery

First read instructions for *Cross Stitch on Afghan Stitch* on page 117. Your background piece has 185 sts (bars) across and 193 rows from bottom to top edge. Embroider center design in **Fig 1** first. Locate center (marked) square on chart; then find center st on your background piece. To find center st, count in from either side to the 93rd st in the 97th row. Thread full strand of light taupe into tapestry needle. Embroider one cross stitch on each side of center st (leave center st unworked). Continue working from center outward until design is completed. Then following chart in **Fig 2,** work border around entire edge, and corner design in each of the outer corners of afghan.

Fringe

Following *Fringe* instructions on pages 9 and 10, make triple knot fringe. Cut 22″ strands of ecru; use 8 strands for each knot of fringe. Tie knots evenly spaced (approx every 5th st) across each short end of afghan. Then work double and triple knots per instructions. Trim ends evenly.

= dk taupe

□ = lt taupe

Fig 1

center
row ●

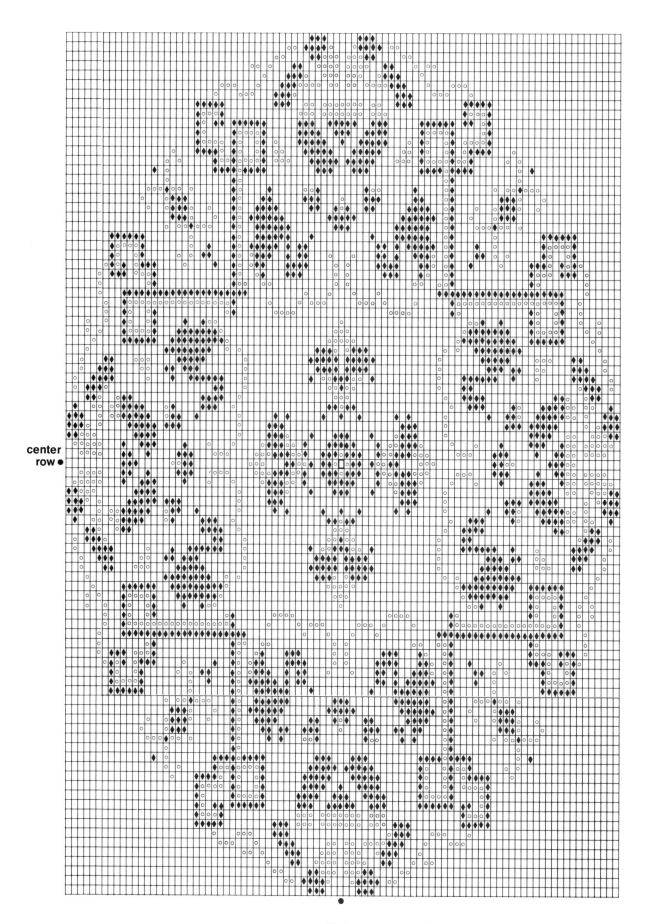

●

126

Fig 2

center
row ●

●center st

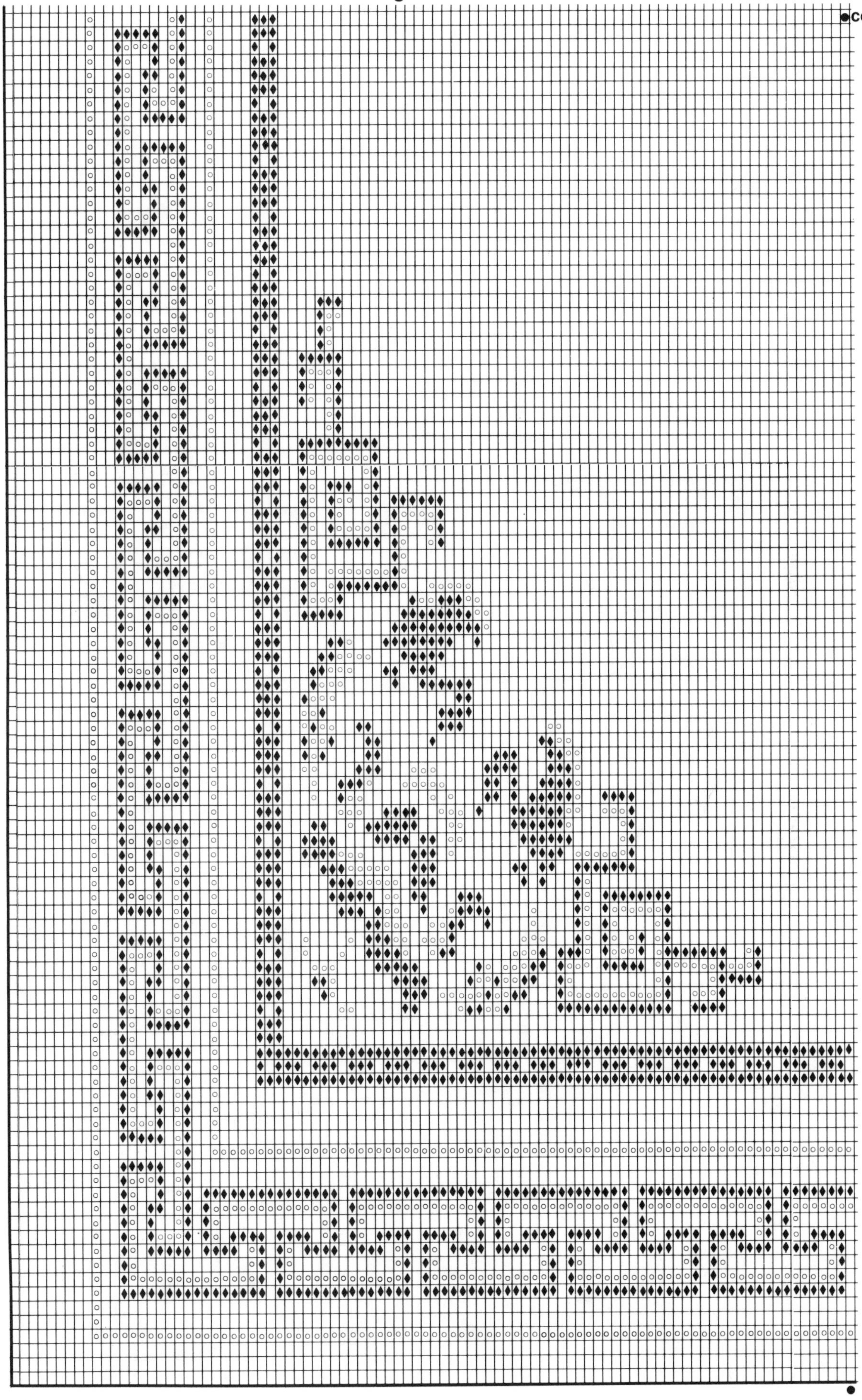

●

afghan stitch
with cross stitch design
MOORISH TILES
designed by Jane Cannon Meyers

SIZE: Approx 49″ x 72″ before fringing

MATERIALS
Worsted weight yarn:
  For afghan: 50 oz antique gold ;
  For embroidery: 2 oz medium yellow;
                          4 oz orange;
                          4 oz dark rust
Size J afghan hook with flexible extension (or size
  required for gauge)
Size 16 tapestry needle (for embroidery)

GAUGE: In afghan st, 4 sts = 1″; 3 rows = 1″

INSTRUCTIONS
With gold, ch 195 *loosely*. Following *Basic Afghan Stitch* instructions on page 116, work 217 rows even in afghan st. At end of last row, bind off (see instructions on page 117).

Embroidery
First read instructions for *Cross Stitch on Afghan Stitch* on page 117. Your background piece has 195 sts (bars) across and 217 rows from bottom to top edge. Using full strand of yarn, embroider design in **Fig 1** as follows. Beg at bottom edge along foundation chain. Leaving one st (bar) at each side edge unworked, work chart across from A to B 3 times; then from A to C once; and work chart up from A to B 5 times; then from A to C once.

Fringe
Following *Fringe* instructions on pages 9 and 10, make triple knot fringe. Cut 25″ strands of gold; use 8 strands for each knot of fringe. Tie knots evenly spaced (approx. every 5th st) across each short end of afghan. Then work double and triple knots per instructions. Trim ends evenly.

Fig 1

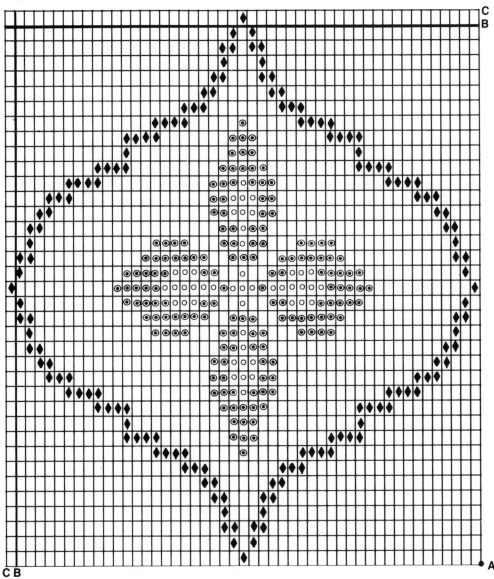

$\boxed{\circ}$ = **yellow**

$\boxed{\odot}$ = **orange**

$\boxed{\blacklozenge}$ = **rust**

afghan stitch
with cross stitch design
SWEET VIOLETS

designed by Jane Cannon Meyers

SIZE: Approx 46″ x 65″ before fringing

MATERIALS
Worsted weight yarn (for afghan): 48 oz white
Persian type crewel yarn (3 ply) for embroidery:
   20 yds yellow;
   10 yds light violet;
   100 yds medium violet;
   56 yds dark violet;
   48 yds light olive green;
   120 yds medium olive green;
   20 yds dark olive green
Size J afghan hook (for size required for gauge)
Size J aluminum crochet hook (for trim and joining)
Size 18 tapestry needle (for embroidery)

GAUGE: In afghan st, 4 sts = 1″; 3 rows = 1″

INSTRUCTIONS

CENTER PANEL
With afghan hook and white, ch 58 *loosely.* Following *Basic Afghan Stitch* instructions on page 116 , work 195 rows even in afghan st. At end of last row, bind off (see instructions on page 117).

Embroidery: First read *Cross Stitch on Afghan Stitch* instructions on page 117 . Panel is 58 sts (bars) across and 195 rows from bottom to top edge. Using full strand of Persian-type yarn, embroider panel as follows. Beg at top along bound-off edge and work chart in **Fig 1** from A to C once; then from B to C twice.

Fig 1

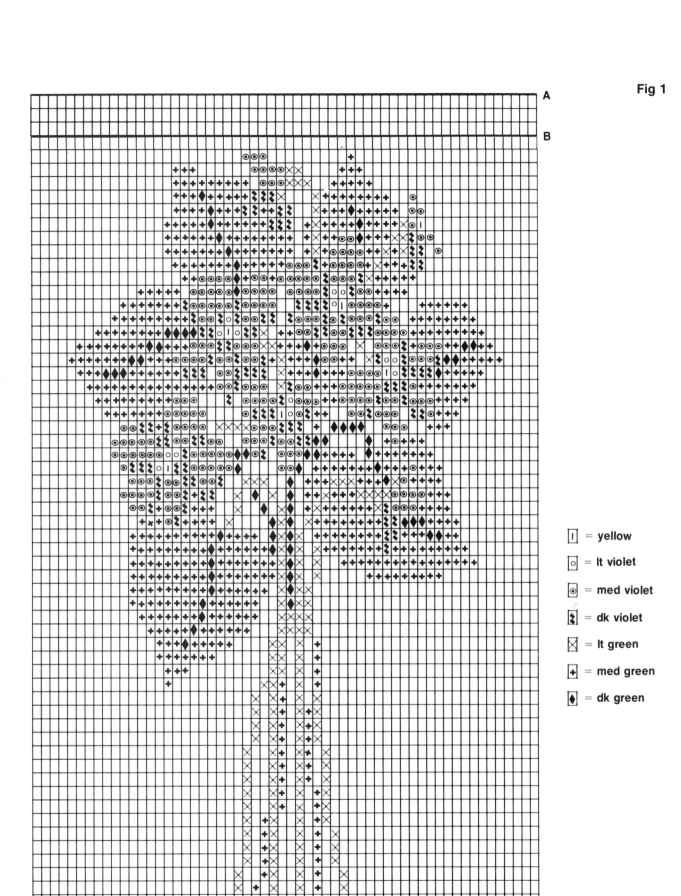

A

B

C

I	= yellow
○	= lt violet
⊙	= med violet
⟨	= dk violet
✕	= lt green
+	= med green
◆	= dk green

SIDE PANEL
(make 4)
With afghan hook and white, ch 20 *loosely*. Work 195 rows even in afghan st. At end of last row, bind off.

Embroidery: Each panel is 20 sts (bars) across and 195 rows from bottom to top edge. Working cross stitches in same manner as Center Panel, beg at top (bound-off) edge and embroider four Side Panels from chart in **Fig 2** as follows. Embroider 2 panels by working chart from A to D three times; then from A to B once. Embroider rem 2 panels by working chart from B to D once; from A to D twice then from A to C once.

PANEL TRIM
(make 5)
Work trim on side edges of each panel as follows.

Left Trim: Hold panel with right side facing, top (bound-off) edge to your right, and side edge across top. With crochet hook, join white with a sl st in last BO st at upper right-hand corner. **Row 1:** Ch 5, sk first 2 rows, hdc in next row; * ch 2, sk next 2 rows, hdc in next row; rep from * across, ending in last row at upper left-hand corner. **Row 2:** Ch 5, turn; * hdc in next hdc, ch 2; rep from * across, ending hdc in 3rd ch of ch-5. Finish off.

Right Trim: Hold same panel with right side facing and edge without trim across top. With crochet hook, join white with a sl st in first row at upper right-hand corner. **Row 1:** Ch 5, * sk next 2 rows, hdc in next row, ch 2; rep from * across, ending hdc in first BO st at upper left-hand corner. **Row 2:** Work same as Left Trim. Finish off; weave in all ends.

Assembling
Place panels side by side, having Side Panel with 7 motifs at each outside edge. To join two panels, hold yarn at back of work and work sl sts on right side, alternating from edge to edge as follows. With crochet hook, join white with a sl st in st at bottom edge of right panel. Insert hook in corresponding st at bottom edge of left panel; hook yarn from beneath work and draw up through work and lp on hook (sl st made). Now work sl st in next st on right panel; then work a sl st in corresponding st on left panel. Continue working in this manner (alternating sl sts from edge to edge) until panels are joined; finish off. Join rem panels in same manner.

Fringe
Following *Fringe* instructions on pages 9 and 10, make triple knot fringe. Cut 25″ strands of white; use 8 strands for each knot of fringe. Tie knots evenly spaced across each short end of afghan. Then work double and triple knots per instructions. Trim ends evenly.

Fig 2

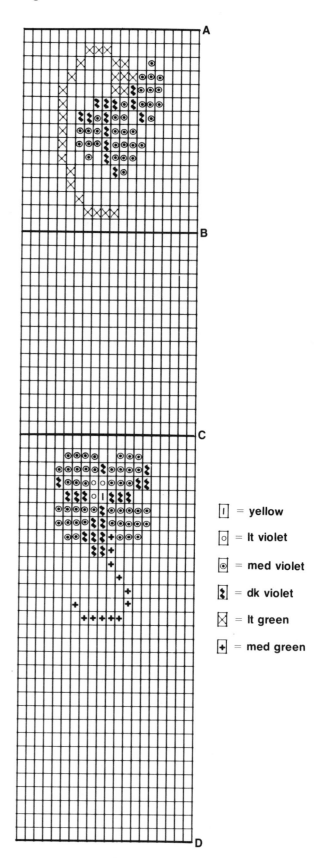

⌶ = yellow

○ = lt violet

◉ = med violet

⧨ = dk violet

⊠ = lt green

⊞ = med green

afghan stitch
SPEARMINT LEAVES

lap robe
designed by Joan Kokaska

SIZE: Approx 23″ x 36″ before fringing

MATERIALS
Worsted weight yarn: 4 oz shamrock green;
**   14 oz spearmint green**
Size J, 14″ afghan hook (or size required for gauge)

GAUGE: In afghan st, 4 sts = 1″; 3 rows = 1″

INSTRUCTIONS
Center Panel
With spearmint, ch 60 *loosely*.

Rows 1 through 7: Following *Basic Afghan Stitch* instructions on page 116, work even in afghan st.
[**Note:** *On following rows, detailed instructions are given for Step 1; to complete row, work Step 2 as given in Basic Afghan Stitch instructions. This will not be mentioned again in instructions.*]

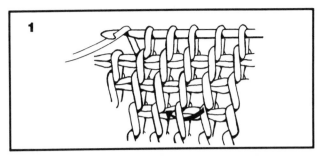

Row 8: Draw up 22 lps (23 lps now on hook). **Work a leaf as follows: YO, draw up a lp under bar which is 2 bars to the right of last lp on hook in 3rd row below (Fig 1), YO and draw through 2 lps on hook (2 lps of leaf now on hook — counting last lp on hook); continue by working the following sts of leaf to the left of st just made; YO twice, draw up a lp under next bar to the left in 4th row below, (YO and draw through 2 lps on hook) twice (3 lps of leaf now on hook); YO 3 times, draw up a lp under next bar to the left in 5th row below (center of leaf), (YO and draw through 2 lps on hook) 3 times (4 lps of leaf now on hook); YO twice, draw up a lp under next bar to the left in 4th row below, (YO and draw through 2 lps on hook) twice (5 lps of leaf now on hook); YO, draw up a lp under next bar to the left in 3rd row below, YO and draw through 2 lps on hook (6 lps of leaf now on hook); YO and draw yarn tightly through all 6 lps = one leaf made.** Return to working row, draw up 14 more lps (37 lps now on hook); work one more leaf, then draw up rem 23 lps across working row.

Rows 9 through 15: [**Note:** *On the next row, be sure to draw up lp under bar at top of leaf.*]. Work 7 rows even in afghan st.

Row 16: Draw up 10 lps (11 lps now on hook), work leaf; draw up 38 more lps across working row (49 lps now on hook), work one more leaf; then draw up rem 11 lps across working row.

Rep Rows 1 through 16, 5 times more; then rep Rows 1 through 8 once. Work 2 more rows even in afghan st; bind off (see instructions on page 117). Weave in all ends.

Side Panel
(make 2)
With shamrock, ch 15 *loosely*.

Rows 1 through 7: Work even in afghan st.

Row 8: Draw up 7 lps (8 lps now on hook); drop shamrock, do not cut. With spearmint, work leaf to last step (6 lps of leaf on hook: 5 lps mint and 1 lp shamrock); cut mint, leaving 4″ end for weaving in later; pick up shamrock, YO and draw through all 6 lps of leaf on hook; draw up rem 7 lps across working row.

Rows 9 through 23: Work 15 rows even in afghan st.

Row 24: Rep Row 8.

Rep Rows 9 through 24, 5 times more. Then work 2 more rows even in afghan st. At end of last row, BO. Weave in all yarn ends.

Joining

With right side facing, hold center panel and right edge side panel, side by side with BO edge of each panel across top. Thread tapestry needle with mint. Beg at top and sew panels tog as follows. Tack yarn securely at top of center panel, then tack again at top of side panel. * Working from side to side, place a small st through middle of edge st on center panel (Fig 2); then place a small st on side panel under the two horizontal threads at edge (Fig 2). Use thumbnail to push seam to back of work. Rep from * down length of afghan; finish off. Join left side panel in same manner, but taking first st in side panel, second st in center panel, etc. Finish off; weave in all ends. Lightly steam press seams if needed.

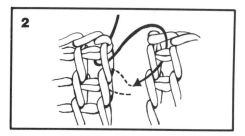

Fringe

Following *Fringe* instructions on page 9, make single knot fringe. Cut 10" strands of mint; use 3 strands for each knot of fringe. Fringe all four sides, tying knots in each st along top and bottom edge, and in each row along sides.

afghan stitch
INDIAN BLANKET

designed by Joan Kokaska

This magnificent afghan features ivory panels with stylized tomahawks, set off by textured rows of edging in charcoal, cranberry and gray.

SIZE: Approx 34" x 58" before fringing

MATERIALS
Worsted weight yarn: 28 oz ivory;
                8 oz cranberry;
                8 oz charcoal heather;
                8 oz light gray heather
Size J, 14" afghan hook (or size required for gauge)
Size J aluminum crochet hook (for panel edging)

GAUGE: In afghan st, 4 sts = 1"; 3 rows = 1"

INSTRUCTIONS

Center Panel
With afghan hook and ivory, ch 25.

Rows 1 and 2: Following *Basic Afghan Stitch* instructions on page 116, work even in afghan st.

Row 3: Draw up a lp under each of next 9 bars (10 lps now on hook); work puff st (abbreviated PS) [**To Work PS: YO, draw up a lp under next bar in 2nd row below (Fig 1); YO and draw through 2 lps on hook; (YO, draw up a lp under same bar in 2nd row below; YO and draw through 2 lps on hook) twice (3 lps of PS now on hook); YO and draw through these 3 lps = PS made.**]; return to working row, draw up a lp under each of next 3 bars; work PS, then draw up a lp under each of rem 10 bars of working row = 25 lps on hook. To complete row on this and all following pattern rows, work Step 2 as given in *Basic Afghan Stitch* instructions.

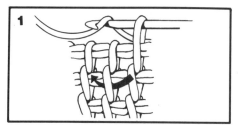

Row 4: Work even in afghan st.

Row 5: (Draw up 4 bars, work PS) twice; draw up 3 bars, work PS; draw up 4 bars, work PS; draw up 5 bars.

Rows 6 through 33: Working from chart in **Fig 2,** beg with Row 6 and work through Row 33.

Fig 2

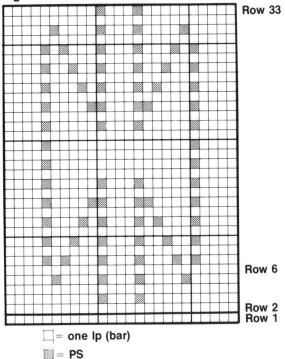

□ = **one lp (bar)**
▨ = **PS**

Rep Rows 2 through 33 of chart in **Fig 2,** 4 times more. You should now have 5 pattern repeats and a total of 161 rows. At end of last row, BO (see instructions on page 117). Weave in all ends.

Right Edging: Hold panel with right side facing, foundation chain edge to your right and side edge across top. With crochet hook, join cranberry with a sl st in ch at upper right-hand corner, ch 1.

Row 1: Sc in same st as joining, dc around 2 horizontal threads of 2nd st from the edge in first row **(Fig 3);** * sc around 2 horizontal threads of first st from the edge in next row; dc around 2 horizontal threads of 2nd st from the edge in next row; rep from * across, ending by working sc in first BO st at upper left-hand corner = 163 sts.

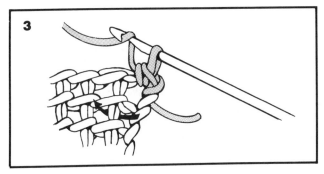

Row 2: Ch 1, turn; sc in each st across = 163 sc.
Row 3: Ch 1, turn; sc in each of first 2 sc; work PS as in panel, but work st around post of next sc in 2nd row below (between dcs) and complete last step of st by working YO and draw through all 4 lps on hook (instead of 3 lps); * sc in next sc, PS around post of next sc in 2nd row below; rep from * to last 2 sc, sc in each of last 2 sc.
Row 4: Rep Row 2. Finish off cranberry.
Row 5: Turn; join lt gray with a sl st in first sc; ch 1, sc in same st as joining; dc around post of next sc in 2nd row below; * sc in next st, dc around post of next sc in 2nd row below (between PS); rep from * to last sc, sc in last sc.
Rows 6 through 8: Rep Rows 2 through 4. At end of Row 4, finish off lt gray.
Row 9: With charcoal, rep Row 5.
Rows 10 and 11: Rep Rows 2 and 3. At end of Row 11, finish off charcoal. Weave in all ends.

Left Edging: Hold same panel with right side facing, BO edge to your right and side edge across top. With crochet hook, join cranberry with a sl st in BO st at upper right-hand corner, ch 1. Work 11 rows of edging in same manner as Right Edging.

Left Side Panel
Work in same manner as Center Panel to Left Edging.
Left Edging: Hold panel with right side facing, BO edge to your right and side edge across top. With crochet hook, join charcoal with a sl st in BO st at upper right-hand corner, ch 1. Work Rows 1 through 4 of Right Edging of Center Panel. Finish off; weave in all ends.

Right Side Panel
Work same as Center Panel to Right Edging. **Right Edging:** Hold panel with right side facing, foundation chain edge to your right and side edge across top. With crochet hook, join charcoal with a sl st in ch at upper right-hand corner, ch 1. Work rows 1 through 4 of Right Edging of Center Panel. Finish off; weave in all ends. **Left Edging:** Work same as Left Edging of Center Panel.

Assembling
Join 2 panels as follows. Place panels side by side with right sides facing you and BO edge of each panel at top. Hold charcoal at back of work and work sl sts on right side, alternating from edge to edge as follows. With crochet hook, join charcoal with a sl st in st at bottom edge of right panel. Insert hook in corresponding st at bottom edge of left panel; hook yarn from beneath work and draw up through work and lp on hook (sl st made). Now work sl st in next st on right panel; then work a sl st in corresponding st on left panel. Continue working in this manner (alternating sl sts from edge to edge) until panels are joined; finish off. Join rem panel in same manner.

Fringe
Following *Fringe* instructions on page 9, make single knot fringe. Cut 14" strands of each color; use 8 strands for each knot of fringe. Matching color of knot to color on afghan, tie knots evenly spaced across each short end of afghan (2 knots at each side charcoal edge, 8 knots at each ivory strip, 2 knots at each cranberry and lt gray strip and 3 knots at each rem charcoal strip).

135

Chapter 8

Kid Stuff

afghan stitch
 with cross stitched design
BEDTIME TALES
designed by Julie A. Ryan

This novel zoo design, whose animals have dimen-
sional tails, should delight children of all ages.

SIZE: Approx 36″ x 46″ before fringing

MATERIALS
Worsted weight yarn:
 For afghan: 18 oz light yellow;
              12 oz light aqua

For embroidery and tails:
      2 yds medium blue;
      ½ oz brown;
      1 oz each white, gold, tan, orange
        and gray ;
      2 oz each light green, dark green
        and black
**Size J afghan hook with flexible extension (or size
 required for gauge)**
Size H aluminum crochet hook (for animal tails only)
Size 16 tapestry needle (for embroidery)

GAUGE: In afghan st, 4 sts = 1″; 3 rows = 1″

INSTRUCTIONS

With afghan hook and yellow, ch 142 *loosely*. Following *Basic Afghan Stitch* instructions on page 116, work 93 rows even in afghan stitch. At end of Row 93, change to aqua. [**To Change Colors: Work Step Two of last row of color being used until 2 lps rem on hook; finish off color being used. With new color, YO and draw through 2 lps on hook (Fig 1) = color changed.**]

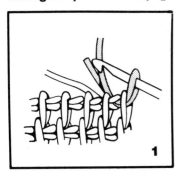

Continuing with aqua, work 45 more rows even in afghan stitch. You should now have 138 rows total. Bind off (see instructions on page 117).

Embroidery

First read instructions for *Cross Stitch on Afghan Stitch* on page 117. Your background piece has 142 sts (bars) across and 138 rows from bottom to top. Using full strand of worsted weight yarn, work cross stitch embroidery from chart in **Fig 2.**

Braided Fringe

Following *Fringe* instructions on page 9, make single knot fringe. Cut 22" strands each of yellow and aqua. Use 4 strands for each knot of fringe. Matching color with afghan (yellow knots along yellow edge and aqua knots along aqua edge), tie 20 groups of 3 knots each (1 st between each of the 3 knots) evenly spaced across each short end of afghan (approx 2 sts between each group). Braid each group of 3 knots and fasten securely approx 4½" from ends of fringe. Trim ends evenly.

Tiger's Tail

[**Color Notes:** *Change colors in last st of old color before new color begins, by working hdc until 3 lps rem on hook; drop color being used (do not cut); with new color, YO and draw through all 3 lps on hook = color changed. Carry color not in use by placing color on top of row and work following sts of new color over it (color will be hidden inside of sts) = color carried.*]

With crochet hook and orange, ch 52. **Row 1:** With orange, hdc in 3rd ch from hook and in each of next 2 chs; with black, hdc in each of next 2 chs; * with orange, hdc in each of next 3 chs; with black, hdc in each of next 2 chs; rep from * across. **Row 2:** With black, ch 2, turn; hdc in next hdc; * with orange, hdc in each of next 3 hdc; with black, hdc in each of next 2 hdc; rep from * to last 2 hdc; with orange, hdc in each of next 2 hdc, hdc in top of ch-2. **Row 3:** With orange, ch 2, turn; hdc in each of next 2 hdc; * with black, hdc in each of next 2 hdc; with orange, hdc in each of next 3 hdc; rep from * to last hdc; with black, hdc in next hdc, hdc in top of ch-2. **Row 4:** Rep Row 2. Finish off, leaving 24" orange sewing length. Sew long edges tog to form a tube; then sew edges on one end of tube tog. Finish off; weave in all ends. Sew open end of tube to afghan (position as shown in photo).

Skunk's Tail

With crochet hook and white, ch 26. Work hdc in 3rd ch from hook and in each rem ch across to last ch; 4 hdc in last ch for round end of tail. Now continue on opposite side of chain and work hdc in each ch across. Finish off, leaving 12" sewing length.

Cut 4" strands of black for fringing tail. Use 2 strands for each knot of fringe. Tie one knot (see *Fringe* instructions on page 9) in each st around, excluding flat end. Sew unfringed end to afghan (position as shown in photo).

Giraffe's Tail

With crochet hook and 3 strands of gold, make a chain to measure 6" long. For tassel at end of tail, wind brown 9 times around 6" length of cardboard; remove cardboard (do not cut yarn). Use 12" strand of gold doubled, and tie strands in half. Attach this folded end to one end of chain securely. Sew opposite end of chain to afghan (position as shown in photo having right side of chain facing afghan).

Zebra's Tail

Cut 4 strands white, each 20" long; then cut 8 strands black, each 20" long. Use 12" strand of black doubled, and tie strands in half. Attach this folded end to afghan securely (position as shown in photo). Divide strands equally into 3 groups — 2 black and 1 white. Braid strands and fasten securely approx 2" from end. Trim ends evenly.

Rabbit's Tail

Wrap white around 3" length of cardboard, 100 times. Remove cardboard (do not cut yarn). Use 12" strand of white doubled, and tie strands in half. Trim ends for a fluffy pompon. Attach securely to afghan (position as shown in photo).

Fig 2

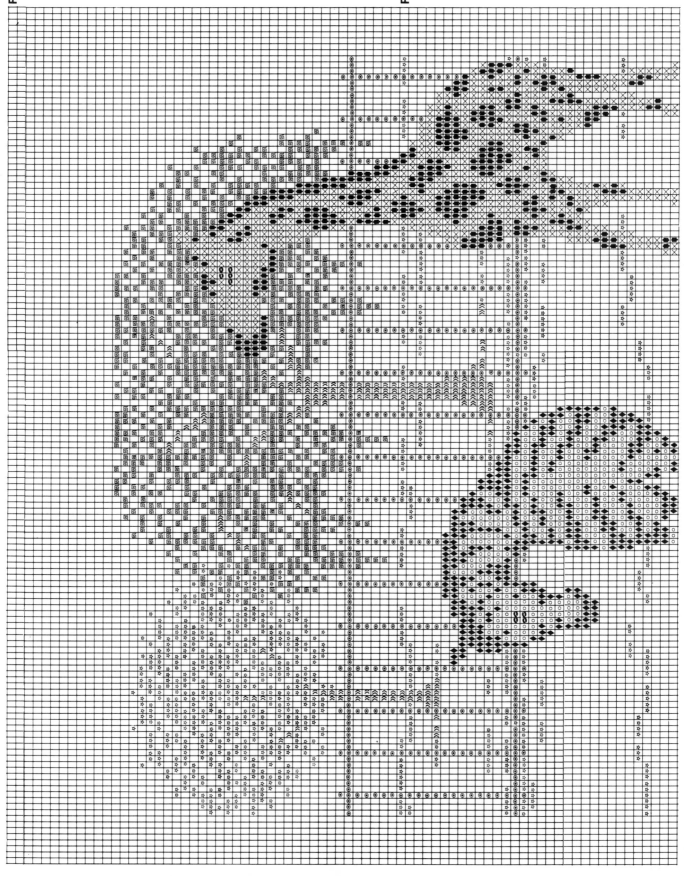

⊡	white
⊠	gold
☑	tan
◖	blue
✚	orange
⊡	lt green
⬚	dk green
◉	gray
▣	brown
◈	black

Row 1

139

crocheted
SUNRISE

designed by Barbara Retzke

SIZE: Approx 33″ x 38″ before fringing

MATERIALS
Worsted weight yarn: 28 oz white;
4 oz yellow;
2 oz orange
Size J aluminum crochet hook (or size required for gauge)

GAUGE: In sc, 3 sts = 1″

INSTRUCTIONS

[**Note:** *Afghan is worked lengthwise.*]

With white, ch 122 *loosely.*

Row 1: Sc in 2nd ch from hook and in each rem ch across = 121 sc.

Row 2: Ch 1, turn; sc in each of first 3 sc; * ch 1, sk one sc, sc in each of next 3 sc; rep from * to last 2 sc; ch 1, sk one sc, sc in last sc.

Row 3: Ch 1, turn; sc in first sc, sc in ch-1, sc in next sc, work a long dc in first skipped sc in 2nd row below [**To Work Long Dc: YO, insert hook in skipped sc in 2nd row below (Fig 1) and draw up a lp to height of working row; (YO and draw through 2 lps on hook) twice = long dc made.**] ; * sk next sc, sc in next sc; sc in ch-1, sc

in next sc; work a long dc in next skipped sc in 2nd row below; rep from * to last 2 sc; sk next sc, sc in last sc.

Row 4: Ch 1, turn; sc in each of first 3 sts, work a long dc in first skipped sc in 2nd row below; * sk next sc, sc in each of next 3 sts; work a long dc in next skipped sc in 2nd row below; rep from * to last 2 sc; sk next sc, sc in last sc.

Rows 5 and 6: Drop white (do not cut); with yellow, rep Row 4, twice. At end of Row 6, finish off yellow.

Rows 7 and 8: With white, rep Row 4, twice.

Rows 9 and 10: Drop white (do not cut); with orange, rep Row 4, twice. At end of Row 10, finish off orange.

Rows 11 and 12: With white, rep Row 4, twice.

Rows 13 and 14: Drop white (do not cut); with yellow, rep Row 4 twice. At end of Row 14, finish off yellow.

Side border is now completed. Continuing with white only, rep Row 4 until afghan measures approx 29″ from beg edge. Then rep Rows 5 through 14, once (for other border). At end of last row, finish off yellow. Continuing with white only, rep Row 4, twice more. **Last Row:** Ch 1, turn; sc in each st across. Finish off; weave in all ends.

Fringe
Following *Fringe* instructions on page 9, make single knot fringe. Cut 16″ strands of each color. Use four strands for each knot of fringe. Tie knots evenly spaced (approx every other row) across each short end of afghan, matching colors with afghan.

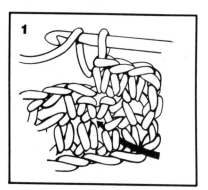

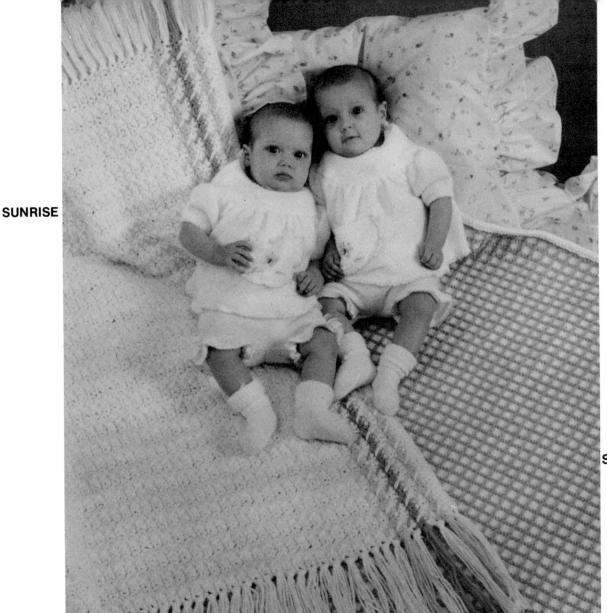

SUNRISE

SPRINGTIME

knitted
SPRINGTIME
designed by Mary Thomas

SIZE: Approx 32″ x 38″

MATERIALS
Worsted weight yarn: 16 oz white;
8 oz lime green
Size 10, 29″ circular knitting needle (or size required for gauge)

GAUGE: In stock st, 4 sts = 1″

INSTRUCTIONS
[**Note:** *Throughout patt, slip each sl st as to purl.*]

With white, CO 147 sts *loosely.* Do not join; work back and forth in rows. Knit 4 rows for garter st border. Finish off white; join green. **Inc Row:** K 11, inc in next st; * K3, inc in next st; rep from * to last 11 sts, K 11 = 179 sts. Now work in pattern stitch as follows.

Row 1: With green, knit in back lp of first st (abbreviated Kb), knit rem sts. Finish off green; join white.

Row 2: With white, K5, sl 1; * K3, sl 1; rep from * to last 5 sts, K5.

Row 3: With white, Kb, K3; P1, sl 1; * P3, sl 1; rep from * to last 5 sts; P1, K4.

Rows 4 and 5: Rep Rows 2 and 3. At end of Row 5, finish off white; join green.

Row 6: With green, knit across.

Rep Rows 1 through 6 until afghan measures approx 37″ from CO edge, ending by working Row 6. **Dec Row:** Continuing with green, Kb, K 10, K2 tog; * K3, K2 tog; rep from * to last 11 sts, K 11 = 147 sts. Finish off green; join white. Knit 4 more rows for garter st border. BO all sts *loosely* in knit. Weave in all yarn ends.

knitted
MORNING GLORY
designed by Mary Thomas

SIZE: Approx 36″ x 42″

MATERIALS
Worsted weight yarn: 16 oz baby blue
Size 11, 29″ circular knitting needle (or size required for gauge)

GAUGE: In garter st, 7 sts = 2″

INSTRUCTIONS
CO 121 sts *loosely*. Do not join; work back and forth in rows. Knit 8 rows for garter st border. Then work in pattern stitch as follows.

Row 1: K7; * YO, K1; sl 1, K1, PSSO; K5, K2 tog; K1, YO, K1; rep from * to last 6 sts, K6. [**Note:** *Each YO counts as one st throughout patt.*]

Row 2: K6, purl to last 6 sts; K6 = 121 sts.

Row 3: K6; * K2, YO, K1; sl 1, K1, PSSO; K3, K2 tog; K1, YO, K1; rep from * to last 7 sts, K7.

Row 4: Rep Row 2.

Row 5: K6; * K3, YO, K1; sl 1, K1, PSSO; K1, K2 tog; K1, YO, K2; rep from * to last 7 sts, K7.

Row 6: Rep Row 2.

Row 7: K6; * K4, YO, K1; sl 1, K2 tog, PSSO; K1, YO, K3; rep from * to last 7 sts, K7.

Row 8: Rep Row 2.

Rep Rows 1 through 8 until afghan measures approx 41″ from CO edge, ending by working Row 7. Then knit 7 more rows for garter st border. BO all sts *loosely* in knit. Weave in all ends.

crocheted
FORGET-ME-NOT
designed by Jean Leinhauser

SIZE: Approx 25½″ x 34″

MATERIALS
Sport weight yarn: 1 oz yellow;
4 oz white;
4 oz blue;
4 oz green
Size G aluminum crochet hook (or size required for gauge)

GAUGE: One square = 3″; one block = 8½″

INSTRUCTIONS

Block (make 12)
With yellow, ch 3.

Rnd 1 (right side): Work 5 hdc in 3rd ch from hook, join with a sl st in top of beg ch-3. Finish off yellow.

Rnd 2: Do not turn; join blue with a sl st in top of ch-3 where prev rnd was joined; work beg puff stitch (PS) in same st [**To Work Beg PS: Ch 3, (YO and draw up ½″ lp in same st) twice (5 lps now on hook); YO and draw through first 4 lps on hook; then YO and draw through rem 2 lps on hook, ch 1 = beg PS made.**]; work PS in same st [**To Work PS: (YO and draw up ½″ lp in st) 3 times (7 lps now on hook); YO and draw through first 6 lps on hook; then YO and draw through rem 2 lps on hook, ch 1 = PS made.**]; work 2 PS in each of rem 5 hdc, join with a sl st in top of beg PS = 12 PS. Finish off blue.

Rnd 3: With right side facing, join green with a sl st in any sp between PS; ch 3, (dc, ch 1, 2 dc) in same sp for first corner; * 2 sc in each of next 2 sps (between PS) for side; work (2 dc, ch 1, 2 dc) in next sp (between PS) for corner; rep from * twice more; 2 sc in each of next 2 sps for last side, join with a sl st in top of beg ch-3. Finish off green.

Rnd 4: With right side facing, join white with a sl st in any ch-1 corner sp; ch 3, (dc, ch 1, 2 dc) in same sp; * ch 1, dc in each of next 4 sc along side; ch 1, work (2 dc, ch 1, 2 dc) all in next ch-1 corner sp; rep from * twice more; ch 1, dc in each of next 4 sc along last side; ch 1, join with a sl st in top of beg ch-3. Finish off white.

Rnd 5: With right side facing, join white with a sl st in any ch-1 corner sp; ch 1, 3 sc in same sp; * sc in each of next 2 dc of corner, sc in ch-1 sp; sc in each of next 4 dc, sc in ch-1 sp; sc in each of next 2 dc of corner, 3 sc in ch-1 corner sp; rep from * twice more; sc in ch-1 sp, sc in each of next 4 dc; sc in ch-1 sp, sc in each of next 2 dc of corner; join with a sl st in beg sc. Finish off white, leaving 14″ sewing length.

One square is now completed. Make three more squares in same manner; then join the four squares to form a block. To join, hold two squares with right sides tog.

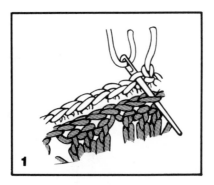

Thread white yarn into tapestry needle and sew tog, working in **outer lps only (Fig 1),** carefully matching sts. Join two more squares in same manner, then join the two pairs of squares, carefully matching sts, corners and seams. Now work edging around joined squares as follows.

Edging
Rnd 1: With right side of joined squares facing you, join green with a sl st in center sc of 3-sc group at any outer corner; work (beg PS, ch 2, PS) in same st; * work (sk one sc, PS in next sc) 6 times across first square, sk joining; PS in center sc of 3-sc group of next square, work (sk one sc, PS in next sc) 5 times; work (PS, ch 2, PS) in center sc of 3-sc group at next outer corner; rep from * twice more; work (sk one sc, PS in next sc) 6 times across square, sk joining; PS in center sc of 3-sc group of next square, work (sk one sc, PS in next sc) 5 times; join with a sl st in top of beg PS. Finish off green.

Rnd 2: With right side facing, join white with a sl st in any corner sp, ch 1; 5 sc in same sp, work sc in each PS and in each sp (between PS) along first side; * 5 sc in next corner sp; work sc in each PS and in each sp (between PS) along next side; rep from * twice more, join with a sl st in beg sc. Finish off white.

Rnd 3: With right side facing, join blue with a sl st in center sc of any 5-sc corner group, ch 1; * 3 sc in center corner st, sc in each sc along side; rep from * 3 times more, join with a sl st in beg sc. Finish off blue.

Rnd 4: With right side facing, join white with a sl st in center sc of any 3-sc corner group, ch 1; * 3 sc in center corner st, sc in each sc along side; rep from * 3 times more, join with a sl st in beg sc. Finish off white.

One block is now completed. Weave in all loose yarn ends.

Finishing
Afghan is 3 blocks wide by 4 blocks long. To join, hold two blocks with right sides tog. Carefully matching sts and corners and working in **outer lps only,** sew blocks into 4 strips of 3 blocks each; then join strips in same manner. Now work one rnd of edging as follows. With right side facing, join white with a sl st in center st of any outer 3-sc corner group, ch 1; * 3 sc in center corner st, sc in each sc along side; rep from * 3 times more, join with a sl st in beg sc. Finish off; weave in all ends. Lightly steam press joinings on wrong side.

crocheted
BABY RICKRACK
designed by Joan Kokaska

An easy pattern in a small ripple design, this afghan is a pleasure to make.

SIZE: Approx 30″ x 42″

MATERIALS
Worsted weight yarn: 20 oz mint green;
6 oz white
Size H aluminum crochet hook (or size required for gauge)

GAUGE: In sc, 7 sts = 2″

INSTRUCTIONS

With white, ch 173 *loosely.*

Row 1 (foundation row): Working **in back ridge** of each ch across **(Fig 1)**, sc in 2nd ch from hook, sk one ch, sc in next ch; 3 sc in next ch, sc in next ch; * sk 2 chs, sc in next ch; 3 sc in next ch, sc in next ch; rep from * to last 2 chs; sk one ch, sc in last ch.

Row 2 (patt row): Ch 1, turn; sc **in both lps** of first sc, sk one sc; working **in back lp only** (lp away from you) of each following sc, sc in next sc, 3 sc in next sc, sc in next sc; * sk 2 sc, sc in next sc; 3 sc in next sc, sc in next sc; rep from * to last 2 sc; sk one sc, sc **in both lps** of last sc.

Rows 3 and 4: Rep Row 2, twice. At end of Row 4, change to green in last sc. [**To Change Colors: Work last sc until 2 lps rem on hook; finish off color being used. With new color, YO and draw through 2 lps on hook = color changed.**]

Rep Row 2 in the following color sequence for striped border: 4 rows each of green, white, green and white. You should now have 20 rows completed. At end of last row of striped border, change to green.

Continue to rep Row 2 (with green only) until afghan measures approx 36″ long. Then work other striped border as follows. Rep Row 2 in the following color sequence: 4 rows each of white, green, white, green and white (20 rows total). At end of last row, finish off; weave in all ends.

knitted
SWEET DREAMS

designed by Mary Thomas

SIZE: Approx 30″ x 42″

MATERIALS
Worsted weight yarn: 20 oz powder blue;
                                    2 oz white
Size 10, 29″ circular knitting needle (or size required
   for gauge)

GAUGE: In stock st, 4 sts = 1″

INSTRUCTIONS

With blue, CO 130 sts *loosely*. Do not join; work back and forth in rows. Work 6 rows even in stock st for hem.

Turning Ridge (right side): Purl across. Now work in pattern as follows;

Row 1 (wrong side): Purl.

Rows 2 through 5: Continuing in stock st (beg with a knit row), work Rows 1 through 4 of chart in **Fig 1.** On knit rows (odd-numbered rows of chart), * work chart from A to B; rep from * across. On purl rows (even-numbered rows of chart), * work chart from B to A; rep from * across. Carry color not in use *loosely* at back of work so as not to "pucker" and distort the design or alter the width of your afghan. At end of Row 5 (Row 4 of chart), finish off white; continue with blue only.

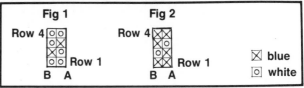

	Fig 1			Fig 2		
Row 4	⊡⊡		Row 4	⊠⊠		
	⊠⊡			⊡⊠		
	⊡⊠			⊠⊡		⊠ blue
	⊡⊡ Row 1			⊠⊠ Row 1		⊡ white
	B A			B A		

Rows 6 and 7: Continuing in stock st, work 2 rows even.

Row 8 (inc row): * Knit in front and back of next st (inc made); rep from * across = 260 sts.

Rows 9 through 15: Beg with a purl row, work 7 rows even in stock st.

Row 16 (dec row): * K2 tog; rep from * across = 130 sts.

Row 17: Purl.

Rows 18 through 21: Continuing in stock st (beg with a knit row), work Rows 1 through 4 of chart in **Fig 2.** At end of Row 21 (Row 4 of chart), finish off white; continue with blue only.

Rows 22 through 32: Rep Rows 6 through 16.

Rep Rows 1 through 32 until afghan measures approx 42″ from turning ridge, ending by working Row 7. **Next Row (right side):** Purl across (for turning ridge). Then beg with a purl row and work 6 more rows even in stock st for hem. BO all sts *loosely* in purl.

Turn hems under and sew *loosely* in place. Weave in all ends. Lightly steam press on wrong side.

knitted
with duplicate stitched design
HAPPY EVENT
designed by Julie A. Ryan

Choose shamrocks or hearts — or create your own design. Knit an afghan for that special event!

SIZE: Approx 36″ square

MATERIALS
Sport weight yarn: 10 oz white;
                    2 oz green (for shamrock design)
                  or red (for heart design)
Size 8, 29″ circular knitting needle (or size required for gauge)
15 Yarn bobbins
Size 16 tapestry needle (for embroidery)

GAUGE: In stock st, 5 sts = 1″; 7 rows = 1″

INSTRUCTIONS
With white, CO 179 sts *loosely.* Do not join; work back and forth in rows. **Row 1:** * K1, P1; rep from * to last st, K1. Rep Row 1, 5 times more for seed st edge. Now work knit-in block design as follows.

Bobbins are used on the next 34 rows for each color change. Wind bobbins as follows: 8 white and 7 green (for shamrock design) or red (for heart design).

Row 1 (right side): Join first white bobbin (finish off ball of white) [**To Join New Color: Tie new color with a knot right up against the needle (Fig 1), leaving approx 4″ end for weaving in later.**] (K1,P1) twice, K1 (for seed st edge); join first green/red bobbin, K 13; * join next white bobbin, K 13; join next green/red bobbin, K 13; rep from * to last 5 sts; join last white bobbin, (K1, P1) twice, K1 (for seed st edge).

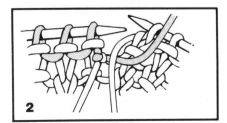

Row 2: With first white bobbin, (K1, P1) twice, K1; with green/red bobbin [**To Change Colors: Bring the color you have just used over and to the left of the color you are going to use, then bring the new color up from underneath (Fig 2) — this twists the two colors**

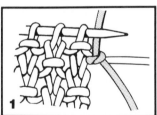

and prevents a hole in your work], P 13; * with white bobbin, P 13; with green/red bobbin, P 13; rep from * to last 5 sts; with last white bobbin, (K1, P1) twice, K1.

Rows 3 through 17: Keeping 5 sts at each end in seed st and colors as established, work 15 more rows in stock st, ending by working a right-side row.

Row 18 (color reverse row): Continuing with first white bobbin (cut off other bobbins, leaving 4″ ends), (K1, P1) twice, K1, P 13; * join green/red bobbin, P 13; join white bobbin, P 13; rep from * to last 5 sts; continuing with white bobbin, (K1, P1) twice, K1.

Rows 19 through 34: Keeping first and last 5 sts in seed st and colors as established, work 16 more rows in stock st, ending by working a wrong-side row.

Cut off all bobbins, leaving 4″ ends. Continue with ball of white only. Work even (keeping 5 sts at each end in seed st and rem sts in stock st) until afghan measures approx 30″ from CO edge, ending by working a wrong-side row. Now work knit-in block design as follows.

Row 1 (right side): Join first white bobbin (finish off ball of white), (K1, P1) twice, K 14; * join green/red bobbin, K 13; join white bobbin, K 13; rep from * to last 5 sts; continuing with white bobbin, (K1, P1) twice, K1.

Rows 2 through 17: Keeping 5 sts at each end in seed st and colors as established, work 16 more rows in stock st, ending by working a right-side row.

Row 18 (color reverse row): Continuing with white bobbin (cut off other bobbins, leaving 4″ ends), (K1, P1) twice, K1; join green/red bobbin, P 13; * join white bobbin, P 13; join green/red bobbin, P 13; rep from * to last 5 sts; join white bobbin, (K1, P1) twice, K1.

Rows 19 through 34: Keeping 5 sts at each end in seed st and colors as established, work 16 more rows in stock st, ending by working a wrong-side row.

Cut off all bobbins, leaving 4″ ends. Continue with ball of white only and work 6 rows in seed st. BO all sts *loosely.* Weave in all yarn ends, being careful to weave each end into back of sts of matching color.

Embroidery
Use duplicate sts **(Fig 3)** and work embroidery as follows.

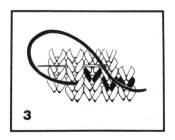

For shamrock design, use white and embroider design in **Fig 4** on each green block at each end of afghan (26 total), having top of each design facing center of afghan. Then with green, embroider design in **Fig 5** on each white block at each end of afghan (26 total) in same manner; and embroider designs in **Figs 4 and 5** in each outer corner of center white section (**see Fig 6** for placement), having top of each design facing center of afghan.

For heart design, use red and embroider design in **Fig 7** on each white block at each end of afghan (26 total), having top of each design facing center of afghan.

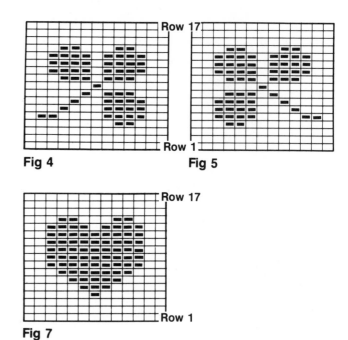

Fig 4   Fig 5

Fig 7

Fig 6

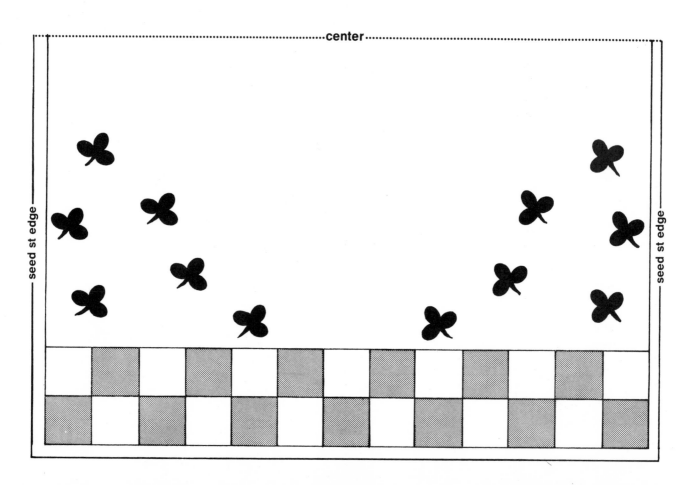

crocheted
SNOWBABY
designed by Joan Kokaska

Designed as a christening blanket, this lovely pattern is made with popcorn and shell stitches.

SIZE: Approx 33″ square

MATERIALS
Sport weight yarn: 14 oz white
Size H aluminum crochet hook (or size required for gauge)

GAUGE: In patt st, 1 shell + 1 PC = 1½″

INSTRUCTIONS
Ch 140 *loosely*.

Row 1: Sc in 2nd ch from hook and in each rem ch across = 139 sc.

Row 2 (right side): Ch 3, turn; 2 dc in first sc (beg ½ shell made); sk next 2 sc, PC (popcorn) in next sc [**To Make PC: Work 4 sc in st; remove hook from lp and insert in first sc of 4-sc group just made, hook dropped lp (Fig 1) and pull through st, ch 1 = PC made.**]; * sk next 2 sc, 5 dc in next sc (shell made); sk next 2 sc, PC in next sc; rep from * to last 3 sc; sk next 2 sc, 3 dc in last sc (½ shell made).

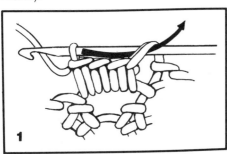

Row 3: Ch 1, turn; sc in first dc, shell (5 dc) in ch-1 at top of next PC; * PC in center dc of next shell [**To Make PC on Wrong Side of Work: Work 4 sc in st; remove hook from lp and insert from back to front in first sc of 4-sc group just made (Fig 2); hook dropped lp and pull through st (pushing sts out to front of work), ch 1 = PC made.**]; shell in ch-1 at top of next PC; rep from * across to ½ shell, sc in top of ch-3 of beg ½ shell.

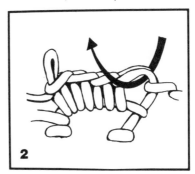

Row 4: Ch 3, turn; 2 dc in first sc (beg ½ shell made), PC in center dc of next shell; * shell in ch-1 at top of next PC, PC in center dc of next shell; rep from * across to last sc, 3 dc in last sc (½ shell made).

Rep Rows 3 and 4 until afghan measures approx 33″ long, ending by working Row 4.

Last Row: Ch 1, turn; work sc in each dc and in each PC across, ending sc in top of ch-3 = 139 sc. Finish off; weave in all ends.

Chapter 9

Specialty Crochet

In this chapter we feature afghans made in two techniques which you may not have tried before: Broomstick Lace and Hairpin Lace. Both require the use of a crochet hook along with another implement: in one case, a single giant knitting needle nearly as thick as a broomstick; in the other, a hairpin lace loom.

Broomstick lace appears to have originated with the Indians of our Southwest, who used an actual broomstick to create the airy, lacy stitches. It is sometimes called Jiffy-Lace.

Hairpin lace, which dates back at least as far as the 1800's, was originally made on a small loom, shaped like a large hairpin, with a fine steel crochet hook. The resulting delicate lace was used to trim collars and cuffs.

Broomstick and hairpin lace are both easy to do, and work up quickly. We hope you'll enjoy trying them.

BROOMSTICK LACE

The following basic instructions apply to all of the lovely broomstick lace designs in this chapter, although each individual pattern will specify the exact number of starting chains, loops and single crochet stitches needed. For practice, use a size 35 broomstick needle and a size H crochet hook.

Basic Instructions

With crochet hook, ch number specified in patt instructions (for practice, ch 20).

Row 1: Draw up lp on hook and place on broomstick needle. Hold broomstick needle in left hand. With crochet hook, and working from left to right across chain, * insert hook in next ch, hook yarn and draw lp through; place lp on broomstick needle **(Fig 1);** rep from * across. Be careful not to twist lps. At end, you should have the same number of lps as number of starting chs. [**Note:** *Lps on broomstick should be firm but not tight.*]

Row 2: Continuing to hold needle in left hand, insert hook in center of first 2 (or number specified in individual patt) lps on needle from right to left **(Fig 2);** sl these 2 lps off needle (leaving lps on hook) as one group; YO and draw lp through, ch 1; now work 2 sc (or same number as lps

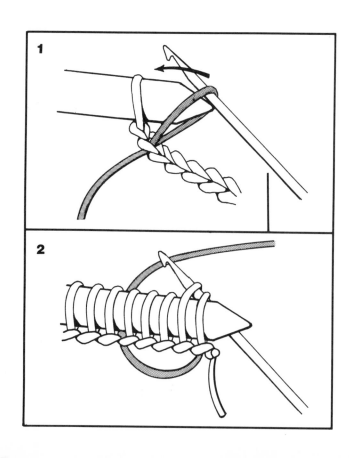

in one group) in center of first group **(Fig 3):** one group made. * Insert hook from right to left through next 2 lps on needle; sl these 2 lps off needle as before, YO and draw lp through, then YO and draw through 2 lps on hook (first sc made); work one more sc in center of same group **(Fig 4):** one more group made. Rep from * across = 20 sc.

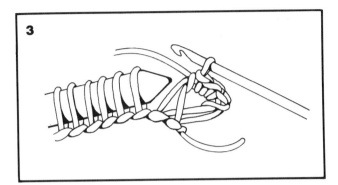

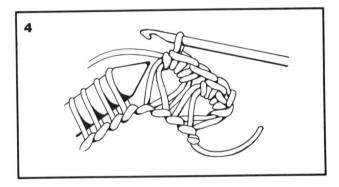

[**Note:** *The number of sc in one group equals the number of lps in one group; and the total number of sc in a row equals the same number of lps in a row or number of starting chs.*]

Row 3: Do not turn; pull up lp on hook and place on needle held in left hand. Working from left to right, sk first sc; * insert hook in **back lp only** of next sc and draw up a lp **(Fig 5);** place lp on needle, being careful not to twist; rep from * across = 20 lps.

Rep Rows 2 and 3 for patt.

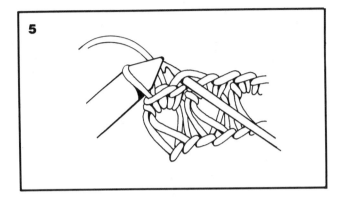

broomstick lace
CANDY MINT
baby afghan

SIZE: Approx 30″ x 36″

MATERIALS
Worsted weight yarn: 4 oz each of pink, mint green and white
Size 35 Boye or Diana Broomstick Lace Needle
Size I Boye or Diana aluminum crochet hook
11 Boye or Diana large yarn bobbins

GAUGE: One group = 1″

INSTRUCTIONS

(Before proceeding, see Basic Instructions on page 150.)

First wind bobbins. Use skeins for outer edges.

With crochet hook and pink, ch 130.

Row 1: Same as Row 1 in *Basic Instructions* = 130 lps.

Row 2: Insert hook in center of first 5 lps on needle; holding these 5 lps tog as one group, sl off needle; YO and draw lp through, ch 1; work 5 sc in center of this group;* work 5 sc in center of next 5 lps; rep from * across = 26 groups.

Row 3: Same as Row 3 in *Basic Instructions* = 130 lps.

Row 4: Rep Row 2.

Row 5: Rep Row 3, working first 10 lps with pink; attach green bobbin (tie yarn into sc where last pink lp was formed) and work next 110 lps; attach pink (skein) and work last 10 lps = 130 lps.

Row 6: Rep Row 2, working pink over pink and green over green. [**To Change Colors: Work last sc of old color until 2 lps rem on hook; drop color being used; with new color, YO and draw through 2 lps on hook = color changed.**]

Now compare your work to the chart in **Fig 1.** You have just completed Patt Rows A, B and C. One Patt Row is made by working 2 rows, Rows 3 and 2. Continue working from the chart only; beg with Patt Row D and work to top of chart, changing colors as indicated. Finish off; weave in all loose ends.

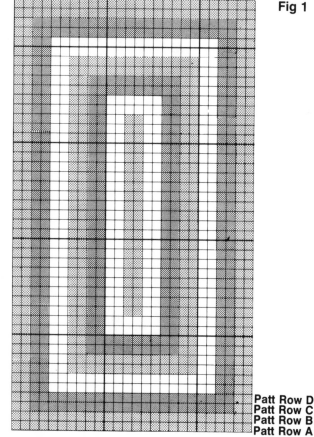

Fig 1

Patt Row D
Patt Row C
Patt Row B
Patt Row A

⊞ white   ▨ pink   ▨ green

broomstick lace
TWO-TONE LACE

SIZE: Approx 47″ x 61″ before fringing

MATERIALS
Worsted weight yarn: 24 oz dark green;
16 oz light green
Size 50 Susan Bates or Marcia Lynn Jiffy-Lace Needle
Size K Susan Bates crochet hook

GAUGE: 2 groups = 2½″; 4 rows (2 groups) = 2½″

INSTRUCTIONS

(Before proceeding, see Basic Instructions on page 150.)

With crochet hook and dk green, ch 204. [**Note:** *Carry color not in use loosely across back of work.*]

Row 1: Draw up last lp on hook and place on needle held in left hand; beg in 2nd ch from hook, draw up a lp in each of next 2 chs and place on needle. Continuing to place each new lp on needle, * with lt green, draw up a lp in each of next 3 chs; with dk green, draw up a lp in each of next 3 chs; rep from * across to last 3 chs; with lt green, draw up a lp in each of last 3 chs = 204 lps.

Row 2: Insert hook in center of first 6 lps on needle; holding these 6 lps tog as one group, sl off needle; with lt green, YO and draw lp through, ch 1, work 2 sc in center of this group; sc in same group, changing to dk green [**To Change Colors: Work sc until 2 lps rem on hook; drop color being used; with new color, YO and draw through 2 lps on hook = color changed.**]; with dk green, work 3 more sc in this same first group, changing to lt green in last sc. Changing colors as before, * work 3 sc with lt green and 3 sc with dk green in next 6 lps; rep from * across = 34 groups.

Row 3: Draw up lp on hook and place on needle held in left hand. Working through **back lps only,** with dk green, draw up a lp in each of next 2 sc and place on needle; with lt green, draw up a lp in each of next 3 sc and place on needle; continuing to place each new lp on needle, * with dk green, draw up a lp in each of next 3 sc; with lt green, draw up a lp in each of next 3 sc; rep from * across = 204 lps.

Rep Rows 2 and 3 until piece measures 61″ long, ending by working Row 2. Finish off.

Side Borders
[**Note:** *Borders are worked with crochet hook only.*]

With right side facing, join dk green at lower right corner with a sl st.

Row 1: Ch 3, sc in base of first group; * ch 3, sc in base of next group; rep from * across long edge.

Row 2: Ch 1, turn; work sc in each sc and 3 sc in each ch-3 sp across.

Row 3: Ch 1, turn; sc in first sc, * ch 1, sk one sc, sc in next sc; rep from * across.

Rows 4 through 11: Ch 1, turn; sc in first ch-1 sp; * ch 1, sc in next ch-1 sp; rep from * across, ending ch 1, sc in sp under turning ch. At end of Row 11, finish off. Work border on opposite side edge in same manner. Steam lightly.

Fringe
Following *Fringe* instructions on pages 9 and 10, work double knot fringe. Cut 18″ strands of dk green; use 10 strands for each knot of fringe. Tie one knot between each group and two knots at each end across each short end of afghan. Tie double knots per instructions.

broomstick lace
RASPBERRY FLIP

SIZE: Approx 48″ x 78″ before fringing

MATERIALS
Worsted weight yarn: 16 oz rapsberry pink;
12 oz medium pink;
12 oz light pink
Size 35 Boye or Diana Broomstick Lace Needle
Size H Boye or Diana crochet hook
2 5 Boye or Diana large yarn bobbins

GAUGE: 2 groups = 2″; 4 rows (2 groups) = 3″

INSTRUCTIONS

(Before proceeding, see Basic instructions on page 150.)
First wind bobbins of each color. With crochet hook and
raspberry pink, ch 250.

Row 1: Same as Row 1 in *Basic Instructions* = 250 lps.

Row 2: Insert hook in center of first 5 lps on needle;
holding these 5 lps tog as one group, sl off needle; YO
and draw lp through, ch 1; work 5 sc in center of this
group; * work 5 sc in center of next 5 lps; rep from * across
= 50 groups.

Row 3: Same as Row 3 in *Basic Instructions* = 250 lps.

Row 4: Rep Row 2.

Row 5: Rep Row 3, working first 10 lps with raspberry pink; attach med pink bobbin (tie yarn into sc where last raspberry pink lp was formed) and work next 230 lps; attach raspberry pink bobbin and work last 10 lps = 250 lps.

Row 6: Rep Row 2, working raspberry pink over raspberry pink and med pink over med pink. [**To Change Colors: Work last sc of old color until 2 lps rem on hook; drop color being used; with new color, YO and draw through 2 lps on hook = color changed.**]

Now compare your work to the chart in **Fig 1.** You have just completed Patt Rows A, B and C. One Patt Row is made by working 2 rows, Rows 3 and 2. Continue working from the chart only; beg with Patt Row D and work to top of chart, changing colors as indicated. Finish off; weave in all loose ends.

Fringe
Following *Fringe* instructions on page 9, make single knot fringe. Cut 7″ strands of each color; use two strands of each color for each knot of fringe. Tie one knot between each group across each short end of afghan.

Fig 1

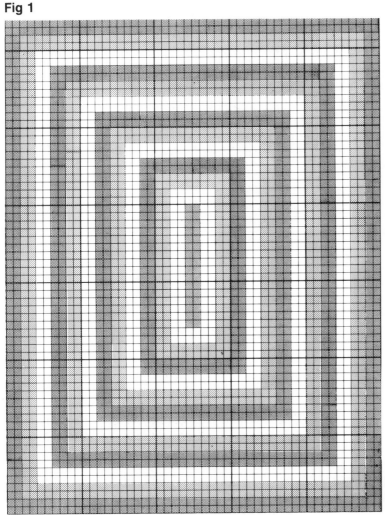

▨ **raspberry pink**

▨ **med pink**

▥ **lt pink**

Patt Row D
Patt Row C
Patt Row B
Patt Row A

broomstick lace

RUFFLES AND LACE

baby afghan

SIZE: Approx 33″ x 37″

MATERIALS
Sport weight yarn: 10 oz baby blue
Size 19 Susan Bates or Marcia Lynn Jiffy-Lace Needle
Size H Susan Bates crochet hook
Satin ribbon ¼″ wide: 5 yds blue

GAUGE: 2 groups = 1″; 4 rows (2 groups) = 1½″

INSTRUCTIONS

Before proceeding, see Basic instructions on page 150.

With crochet hook, ch 120.

Row 1: Same as Row 1 in *Basic Instructions* = 120 lps.

Row 2: Insert hook in center of first 2 lps on needle; holding these lps tog as one group, sl off needle; YO and draw lp through, ch 1; work 2 sc in center of this group; * work 2 sc in center of next 2 lps; rep from * across = 60 groups.

Row 3: Same as Row 3 in *Basic Instructions* = 120 lps.

Rep Rows 2 and 3 until 45 patt repeats are completed, ending by working Row 2. Do not finish off; continue with ruffle.

Ruffle

Row 1: Pull up lp on hook and place on needle held in left hand. Working from left to right, insert hook in **front lp only** of first sc and draw up a lp, place lp on needle (inc made); * insert hook in back lp only of next sc and draw up a lp, place lp on needle; insert hook in front lp only of same sc and draw up a lp, place lp on needle (inc made); rep from * across = 240 lps.

Row 2: Same as Row 2 of afghan = 120 groups.

Row 3: Rep Row 1 of Ruffle = 480 lps.

Row 4: Same as Row 2 of afghan = 240 groups. Finish off.

Work 4 rows of Ruffle across opposite end, picking up 2 lps in each ch across (240 lps). Then work 4 rows on each side edge as follows. Pick up 266 lps across and place on needle; then work Rows 2 through 4 of Ruffle. You should have 133 groups at end of Row 2; and 266 groups at end of Row 4.

Sew all four corners tog. Beg in one corner and weave ribbon through beg group row of ruffle around afghan. Tie ends into a bow.

HAIRPIN LACE

Hairpin lace is a form of crochet in which yarn is looped around two parallel bars, and a center braid of crochet worked up the middle. The width of the lace is determined by the distance between the bars. Hairpin lace looms (or forks) come in several widths, or adjustable frames which can be used for a variety of widths.

BASIC INSTRUCTIONS

[**Note:** *The loom is always held in a vertical position.*]

Step 1: Place strand of yarn from ball on flat surface such as a table, and lay loom across yarn **(Fig 1).**

Step 2: Bring yarn end and yarn from ball to center of loom and tie tightly over bottom strand, allowing approx 8″ of yarn to hang free **(Fig 2).** Tie a small knot at end of the free yarn to indicate bottom of strip (for joining strips later).

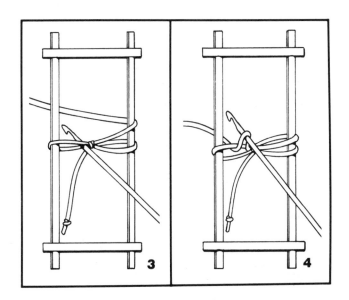

Step 3: Hold loom in left hand; bring ball yarn around right bar to back of loom. Insert hook between the two threads of the loop directly to the left of center knot **(Fig 3).**

Step 4: Hook yarn and bring loop through **(Fig 4),** ch 1.

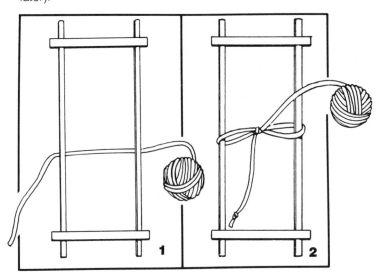

Step 5: To get hook in position for next step, keep loop on hook and pass handle of hook between the two bars and through to back of loom **(Fig 5).** Turn loom to the left ½ turn (opposite side now facing you); yarn will wind around bar as it is turned.

Step 6: Insert hook between the two threads of the top loop directly to the left of center knot **(Fig 6)** and work one sc (YO and draw loop through; YO and draw through 2 loops on hook).

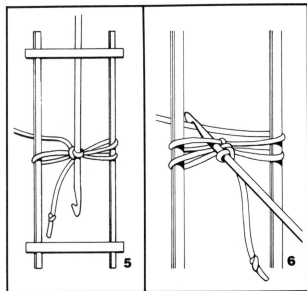

Rep Steps 5 and 6 for desired number of loops. Always count loops carefully, being sure that you have the same number on each side of the loom. To finish off a strip, cut yarn, leaving approx 6″ end; then draw end through loop on hook. Do not cut; leave end for securing last loops in joining strips later.

HELPFUL HINTS

1. Centering Braid: At first you may have a tendency to pull your work too tightly toward one side or the other as you work the single crochet, causing the center braid to lean toward one side. Work slowly and carefully in the beginning, and make a strong effort to keep the braid centered.

2. Full Loom: Remove bottom bar and slip off as many loops as needed. Replace bar and roll up strip; secure strip to bottom of loom with a medium stitch holder or a rubber band.

3. Gauge: Gauge is measured along the center braid, while the work in *on* the loom. If you get more stitches than specified, change to a larger size crochet hook; if you get less stitches than specified, change to a smaller size hook.

4. Counting Loops: When a large number of loops are required, use a marker (stitch marker or a piece of contrasting yarn) and mark every 25th or 50th loop on each bar.

hairpin lace
LIGHT AND LOVELY

SIZE: Approx 40″ x 60″

MATERIALS
Worsted weight yarn: 20 oz white;
                4 oz each of green, purple
                and peacock
Susan Bates or Marcia Lynn Adjustble Hairpin Lace
   Loom
Size H Susan Bates crochet hook (or size required for
   gauge)
Materials Note: Yarn is used doubled throughout
   patt.

GAUGE: 9 sc = 5″, measured at center of strip

INSTRUCTIONS
Adjust loom to 3″ width. [**Note:** *Throughout patt, 2 strands of same color yarn are held tog; each loop of lace has two strands of yarn, and is counted as one loop.*]

Following *Basic Instructions* on page 157, make 10 strips of white, and 3 strips each of green, purple and peacock, having 106 lps on each side of loom.

Assembling
Strips are joined in the following color sequence: white, *green, white, purple, white, peacock, white; rep from * twice more. Join first 2 strips as follows. Place one white and one green strip side by side on a flat surface, having white strip to your right and bottom of each strip toward you. Beg at bottom of strips and being careful not to twist lps, insert hook in first lp of white strip, pick up first lp of green strip and draw through white loop; * pick up next lp of white strip and draw through green loop; pick up next lp of green strip and draw through white loop; rep from * until strips are joined. Secure last lp with strand at end of strip. Join rem strips in same manner.

Border
With 2 strands of white, make a sl loop on hook and join with a dc in first 2 lps on long free edge of a white strip; ch 1 loosely, dc in top of dc just made, dc in same 2 lps as joining; * dc in next 2 lps, ch 1 loosely; dc in top of dc just made, dc in same 2 lps (1 patt made); rep from * in each group of 2 lps to next corner; make 2 patts in corner 2 lps. Continue across short edge, working one patt in each center braid of each strip and in each joining. Work rem sides and corners in same manner, ending by working one patt in beg corner. Join with a sl st in beg dc; finish off. Weave in all ends.

hairpin lace
PEEK-A-BOO

baby afghan

SIZE: Approx 30″ x 35″

MATERIALS
Susan Bates Softura Baby Yarn, or Pompadour Yarn, in 50-gm balls: 8 balls blue;
                            1 ball white
Susan Bates or Marcia Lynn Adjustable Hairpin Lace Loom
Size G Susan Bates crochet hook (or size required for gauge)
Materials Note: Yarn is used doubled throughout patt.

GAUGE: 5 sc = 1″, measured at center of strip

INSTRUCTIONS
Adjust loom to 2″ width. [**Note:** *Throughout patt, 2 strands of yarn are held tog; each lp of lace has two strands of yarn, and is counted as one lp.*]

Following *Basic Instructions* on page 157, make 10 strips of blue, with 120 lps on each side. Work a picot edging on both sides of each strip as follows. Beg at bottom of strip and keeping one twist in all lps throughout, make a sl loop on hook with blue (remember to use 2 strands); join with a sc in first 2 lps; ch 2, sc in same lps as joining (first picot made); * (sc, ch 2, sc) in next 2 lps (picot made); rep from * across. Finish off. Beg at top of strip and work in same manner along opposite side.

Joining Strips
To join, place two strips side by side, with right sides facing you and bottom edge of each strip toward you.

Join blue (remember to use 2 strands) with a sl st in first picot at bottom edge of right strip; ch 2, sl st in first picot of left strip; * ch 2, sl st in next picot of right strip; ch 2, sl st in next picot of left strip; rep from * until strips are joined. Join rem strips in same manner.

Short End Edgings

Working along one short end of afghan, with right side facing, make a sl loop on hook with blue; join with a sc in sc of long edge at corner, ch 2 (mark this ch for corner); sc in same st as joining (beg picot made); picot (sc, ch 2, sc) in loop to right of center braid of first strip, picot in center braid and in loop to left of center braid of same strip; * work 3 picots evenly spaced over joining of strips and 3 picots over next strip (same manner at first strip); rep from * across, ending by working picot in first sc on long edge (mark ch-2 of this picot for corner). Finish off. Work edging along opposite short end of afghan in same manner.

Border

With blue, make a strip with 504 lps on each side. Work a picot edging on both sides of strip as follows. **Inner Edge:** Beg at top of strip; use 2 strands of blue and work picot as before in first 6 lps, picot in next 7 lps, picot in next 6 lps (first corner made); * (picot in next 2 lps) 48 times; picot in next 6 lps, picot in next 7 lps, picot in next 6 lps (next corner made); (picot in next 2 lps) 59 times; picot in next 6 lps, picot in next 7 lps, picot in next 6 lps (next corner made); rep from * once more, ending last rep without working corner; join with a sl st in beg sc, being careful not to twist strip. Finish off. **Outer Edge:** With right side facing, use 2 strands of white and work picot edging in same manner as on joined strips of afghan, join with a sl st in beg sc. Finish off; join center of strip tog.

Joining Border: Place inner edge of border next to afghan, with right sides facing you and carefully matching corners and sides. Beg at short end of afghan and border; join 2 strands of blue with sl st in corner picot of afghan; **ch 2, sl st in 7-lp group of border; ch 2, sl st in same picot of afghan; * ch 2, sl st in next picot of border; ch 2, sl st in next picot of afghan; rep from * to next corner picot of afghan; ch 2, sl st in corner picot of afghan; rep from ** around, join with a sl st in beg st. Finish off; weave in all ends.